The Way of Pilgrimage is like a new best friend! You can walk right into its welcoming presence and begin at once to find fresh truths sprouting up from ancient sources. It will become a trusted guide for those who accompany youth and young adults on their paths of meaning-making.

It promises especially satisfying moments for leaders who wish to engage others in the rhythmic paces of spiritual formation. The weekly gatherings show us how to move from deeply ingrained habits of content-based Bible study into soul-tending practices of contemplation and community that open us to transformation.

—THE REVEREND DR. DORI BAKER
Author, *Doing Girlfriend Theology: God-Talk with Young Women*
United Methodist pastor and professor of youth ministry and Christian education

As an organization completely dedicated to the art of pilgrimage, we are overjoyed with *The Way of Pilgrimage* resources. *The Way of Pilgrimage* is a comprehensive and passionate guide that brings us back to our ancient heritage of pilgrimage through modern eyes and practical application.

Utilize these resources to teach your youth God's unique design of our lives as journeys of exploration and adventure. There is no better resource available to date that prepares your teens as lifelong pilgrims.

—SHAWN SMALL
Executive director, Wonder Voyage Pilgrimages

Finally—a spiritual resource for youth and young adults with depth and meaning! Upper Room Books continues its Companions in Christ series with an insightful and creative journey for Generation Next. I love this resource!

—BO PROSSER
Coordinator for congregational life, Cooperative Baptist Fellowship

This inspiring resource meets participants wherever they are in their spiritual walk and gently moves them toward a deeper understanding of their own pilgrimage. In the context of a Christian community of travelers, participants shed light on the most unexamined corners of their souls. . . .

As an educator of secondary students, I greatly appreciate how consistently this text works to provide spiritual development activities for every kind of learner—from still meditation to verbal expression to artistic interpretations.

—JESSICA ROSENTHAL
United Methodist educator and youth helper

The Way of Pilgrimage is a wonderful doorway into the spiritual life. Like the bountiful feast that God sets before us, these volumes are full of wisdom and blessing. Those who accept the challenge to walk with Christ will benefit greatly from this guide. Its exercises are both simple and rich. At every point, the members of the group are encouraged to journey into the heart of God.

—THE REVEREND DANIEL WOLPERT
Pastor, First P̶r̶e̶s̶b̶y̶t̶erian Church, Crookston, Minn.
Codirecto̶r̶ ̶ ̶ ̶ ̶ ̶ ̶ ̶ ̶ ̶ ̶ ̶ ̶ contemplation and Healing (MICAH)
Author, *Leading a Life with God*

LEADER'S GUIDE

A COMPANIONS *in Christ* Resource

LEADER'S GUIDE

Sally Chambers
Jonathon Norman
Gavin Richardson

UPPER
ROOM BOOKS®
NASHVILLE

THE WAY OF PILGRIMAGE
Leader's Guide

Cover design: Left Coast Design, Portland, OR
Interior design: Gore Studio, Inc., Nashville, TN
Typesetting: PerfecType, Nashville, TN
First printing: 2007

ISBN-13:   978-0-8358-9827-0
ISBN-10:   0-8358-9827-X

LIBRARY OF CONGRESS-CATALOGING-IN-PUBLICATION DATA
Chambers, Sally.
   The way of pilgrimage : leader's guide / Sally Chambers, Jonathon Norman, and Gavin Richardson.
      p. cm.
   Includes bibliographical references.
1.   Church group work with youth. 2. Spiritual formation.   I. Norman, Jonathon. II. Richardson, Gavin. III. Title.
   BV4447.C43 2006
      263',041—dc22

                                                                2005025541

Printed in the United States of America

CONTENTS

VOLUME 4
COMPANIONS ON THE PILGRIMAGE, 117

VOLUME 5
STEPPING INTO THE WORLD, 149

ACKNOWLEDGMENTS

The Way of Pilgrimage is a new adventure in spiritual formation for the rising generation of Companions in Christ groups. The original Companions in Christ twenty-eight-week resource was published by Upper Room Books in spring 2001. The ensuing Companions in Christ series has been designed to create settings in which people can respond to God's call to an ever-deepening communion and wholeness in Christ—as individuals, as members of a small group, and as part of a congregation.

The Way of Pilgrimage stands on the shoulders of all those who created, developed, and wrote the Companions in Christ foundational resource. These writers are named in the acknowledgment section of that initial resource. Special thanks go to Stephen Bryant, whose vision of small groups as important settings for spiritual formation provided inspiration for the Companions in Christ series. Stephen wrote all the daily exercises in *The Way of Pilgrimage* Participant's Books.

The original Companions in Christ material was tested with two senior high groups from St. Paul's Episcopal Church in Franklin, Tennessee (led by Robin Pippin) and St. George's Episcopal Church, Nashville, Tennessee (led by Christy Beesley). Insights from these two groups helped immensely in the formation of this new resource.

Building upon the Companions in Christ foundational vision, *The Way of Pilgrimage* is written for a younger audience of senior-high youth and first-year college students. Many youth and young adults contributed to the shaping of this resource.

The first consultation for developing *The Way of Pilgrimage* was held in Nashville in February 2005. This small group significantly shaped the content and format of this new resource, and some of them became its writers. We are deeply grateful to these participants and to the writers of the Leader's Guide and Participant's Books: Sally Chambers, Kyle Dugan, Steve Matthews, Craig Mitchell, Jeremy Myers, Jonathon Norman, Kara Lassen Oliver, Gavin Richardson, Ciona Rouse, Jessica Rosenthal, Daniel Wolpert, and Jenny Youngman.

We are also indebted to the reviewers of the early manuscript who offered their insights on theology and pilgrimage: The Reverend Matthew Corkern, Christ Church Cathedral Episcopal Church, Nashville, Tennessee; Sally Chambers, St. Paul's Episcopal Church in Franklin, Tennessee; and Jeremy Myers, Augsburg College, Minneapolis, Minnesota.

The Companions in Christ staff team worked diligently to support, review, and revise this resource: Stephen Bryant, Sharon Conley, Lynne Deming, Janice Neely, Robin Pippin, Kathleen Stephens, and Marjorie Thompson. Other staff readers included Catherine Shell, Jay Clark, Bill Lizor, Julie O'Neal, and Tony Peterson.

The following churches and groups tested portions of early versions of *The Way of Pilgrimage* in 2005 and 2006:

Belmont United Methodist Church, Nashville, Tennessee
    leader: Jessica Rosenthal

Wesley United Methodist Church, Coral Gables, Florida
    leader: The Reverend César J. Villafaña

First United Methodist Church, Hendersonville, Tennessee
    leader: Gavin Richardson

North Park University, Chicago, Illinois
    leaders: Susan Braun and Jodi DeYoung

Milford United Methodist Church, Milford, Michigan
    leader: Sherry Foster

Westminster Presbyterian Church, Eugene, Oregon
    leaders: Jen Butler and Katie Stocks

St. Paul's Episcopal Church, Richmond, Virginia
    leader: Steve Matthews

SoulFeast 2006 Youth Program in Lake Junaluska, North Carolina
    leader: Ciona Rouse

Special gratitude to Sally Chambers, who embodies the word *pilgrim* and passionately invites young people to the pilgrimage adventure; and to Kara Oliver, who lent her knowledge of youth ministry, editing skills, and common sense to see the project to completion.

—*The Companions in Christ Staff Team*
Upper Room Ministries

MEET THE WRITERS

SALLY CHAMBERS was born in England and moved to Ohio at the age of ten. She received her BS in human development and social policy from Northwestern University and earned her master's degree in clinical social work from Ohio State University. For the past sixteen years, Sally has been involved with youth ministry. She is entering her tenth year as youth minister at St. Paul's Episcopal Church in Franklin, Tennessee.

God has blessed Sally with a love of reading, photography, art, and music. They, along with her dog, Doodlebug (where she goes, he goes), are her means of nurture outside the church. She regularly takes retreats and strives to follow the monastic cycle of prayer throughout each day. She is a full-time pilgrim herself, as well an experienced leader for others making pilgrimage.

JONATHON NORMAN is minister to and with youth at Hermitage United Methodist Church in Nashville, Tennessee, and the author of *Worship Feast Readings: Fifty Readings, Rituals, Prayers and Guided Meditations.* He is the cofounder and worship leader for the InSearchOf Worship Community, a missional worship group rooted in contemplative styles of worship and prayer. In addition to full-time youth ministry and writing, Jonathon is currently working on a master of theology degree.

GAVIN RICHARDSON is youth minister at First United Methodist Church in Hendersonville, Tennessee. He is a twelve-year veteran of youth ministry. He has spent years working in various capacities in camps and churches in the south and northeast, sits on the board of The Edge Ministries, and is cofounder of the InSearchOf Worship Community. Gavin has collaborated on youth ministry resources with both The United Methodist Publishing House and Upper Room Ministries.

PREFACE

We Are a Pilgrim People

We are a people who are always moving, always wanting more, never satisfied, never full, and never finished. Go back to the Garden and see that we were created with pilgrim hearts: hearts to know, hearts to love, hearts to seek and glorify the God who made us and continues to walk with us.

This desire has not changed. Life this side of Eden may be far busier and more distracted, incredibly more difficult, and not nearly as beautiful, but our hearts are still the same. And as Saint Augustine in the fourth century so truthfully prayed: "You have made us for yourself, O Lord, and our heart is restless until it rests in you." We have hearts that will never rest, never be satisfied, never be complete until we find the God who is at the core of all we desire and seek through this life. And so we journey on in our search.

Throughout the scriptures God constantly reminds people of their pilgrim hearts and calls them back to the path that leads them home. The psalmist declares, "For I am . . . a traveler passing through, as my ancestors were before me" (Ps. 39:12, NLT). And the letter to the Hebrews says it quite simply: We are "strangers and pilgrims on the earth" (11:13, NKJV). The word *pilgrim* literally comes from the Latin word meaning "resident alien." This world is not our home. Our life here on earth is just one stop on this all-encompassing pilgrimage, a physical and spiritual journey home to the One to whom we truly belong. We are a pilgrim people.

Since all are called to pilgrimage (though no two journeys are the same), how do we remember what we have forgotten about who we are and the journey we are on? Without traveling far and wide, how do we awaken our pilgrim hearts? Pilgrimage in its purest and most traditional form is not about the destination but the journey itself. It is not about where we travel but how we travel. Pilgrimage is a journey made on the outside to mark a journey on the inside. Ultimately, pilgrimage moves us toward the One we seek. So although the beauty, adventure, and excitement of leaving home physically on pilgrimage are alluring, they are not essential. We are a pilgrim people whether we leave home or not.

In your hands you hold the map for each of five six-week pilgrimages, but before you begin, here are a few reminders for the road:

- *You, as a leader, are yet another pilgrim on this journey.* Even pilgrimage guides are pilgrims at heart and in practice. This journey doesn't need chaperones.

- *There is a difference between being a tourist and being a pilgrim.* Just as we can travel to holy places as a tourist, not fully engaged or fully present, we also can walk this spiritual pilgrimage of faith as a tourist. Tourists may take snapshots of places along the way and yet keep their hearts far removed, offering empty words to those they meet. Tourists also may be here only for the community and not the journey. *This is a journey for pilgrims.*

- *Companions along the way are essential to pilgrimage.* As fellow pilgrims we journey side by side, looking out together for the One we seek. We need one another for comfort, support, and accountability. Keep in mind, however, that even though we travel with others, each pilgrim must make his or her own journey.

- *Each weekly gathering is a stop along the way.* Each gathering is space carved out and made holy. When we gather together, the gateway between God and us seems to open, and the intersection of heaven and earth become more apparent. Each gathering is a place that says, *Welcome, pilgrims. Welcome to this respite. Welcome to this holy place.*

- *Our journey involves being alert for the movement of the Holy Spirit.* We are learning to follow the guidance of the Holy Spirit, and this takes flexibility. Therefore, if a particular exercise or format doesn't seem to work with your group, change it to make it work. If you feel nudged to do something a different way, then follow where God leads you on this journey. What you hold here is a map. As with any map, there may be several alternative routes that lead to the same place.

- *Rhythm is part of the daily routine of pilgrims.* In medieval times, pilgrims would set out on their journey in exactly the same way. Ritual and repetition were intrinsic to pilgrimage. And because pilgrims followed the same path, we can follow medieval pilgrim trails today in Europe and in the Holy Land. Every Good Friday pilgrims walk the way of the cross, the same path Jesus walked to his death (according to tradition). Repetition and rhythm are essential parts of the spiritual life. So stick with it, and you will find that particular prayers, scriptures, and practices repeated through the journey will begin to sink from your head down to your heart; they will become as familiar and comforting as wearing a favorite old pair of shoes.

- *Practice time happens between gatherings.* The in-between time (days between the weekly gatherings) is practice time. Here we begin to see that the gates of heaven are everywhere, and we ourselves are holy ground where heaven and earth intersect.

- *Pilgrimage is about being present in the present.* This pilgrimage is about waking up and paying attention to our lives. It also involves remembering our past. As we learn to live our days in ceaseless prayer, we will more and more become present to God and to all of life.

- *This is a journey of the heart as well as the head.* In this journey, prayer, conversation, listening, reading, noticing, and looking are transformed from activities of the mind to practices of the heart.

So welcome, pilgrim! May you journey faithfully and with integrity. May you make great strides, though this pilgrimage does not literally go far. Even as you guide others on this way, may your heart also be awakened to who you really are and what you truly seek. And may Christ "dwell in your hearts through faith, as you are being rooted and grounded in love. . . . May [you] have the power to comprehend, with all the saints, what is the breadth and length and height and depth, and to know the love of Christ that surpasses knowledge, so that you may be filled with all the fullness of God" (Eph. 3:17-19).

Welcome home. Welcome to *The Way of Pilgrimage.*

—*Sally Chambers*

INTRODUCTION

Welcome to *The Way of Pilgrimage*, a Companions in Christ resource designed especially for senior-high youth and first-year college students. The purpose of this small-group guide is the same as all the Companions in Christ resources: to create settings in which people can respond to God's call to an ever-deepening communion and wholeness in Christ—as individuals, members of a small group, and part of a congregation or larger faith community.

About the Resource and Process

The Participant's Books contain daily exercises and brief articles to read five days per week prior to a group meeting.

The Leader's Guide gives instruction for this weekly hour-and-fifteen-minute meeting. Each weekly gathering uses a similar structure: time for *Welcoming* pilgrims to the space; *Noticing* how God has been present in their week; moving the theme or message of the week from *Head2Heart* through an experiential group spiritual practice; *Naming* their experience of God's presence in the group practice; and *Blessing and Sending Forth* on the journey.

Each of the five volumes in *The Way of Pilgrimage* contains six weeks of content, for a total of thirty-one weeks, including the introductory meeting. Each volume can be used alone or in combination with one or more of the others. We recommend using the volumes in their numbered order, but that is not essential. A Closing Pilgrimage and Retreat model can be found at www.companionsinchrist.org/leaders.

The volumes are:

1. *Choosing Pilgrimage:* In this volume we are invited to hear the call to be on pilgrimage by contemplating Jesus' baptism and the means of grace. We take a look at the "faces" of God's grace in scripture and in the stories of Christians through the ages who have awakened to grace. We also recognize the hindrances to being on pilgrimage. We acknowledge pilgrimage as a journey home to the heart of God.

2. *The Bible: Pilgrimage Travel Guide.* We are introduced to scripture as guide for the pilgrimage, as the story of fellow pilgrims, and as a place to make our home through study, individual meditation, directed imagination, and group meditation.

3. *Prayer: Heart of the Pilgrimage.* This unit is at the heart of the resource because a pilgrim's prayer leads to the heart of God. Prayer becomes a central activity for a pilgrim. For a model we look to the prayer life of Jesus. Other topics covered are impediments to prayer, the Psalms as prayer guide, prayer methods, and creative ways to pray.

4. *Companions on the Pilgrimage.* The cloud of witnesses who have gone before, as well as present-day pilgrims, accompany us. This volume explores spiritual friendship, spiritual direction and mentoring, small groups, walking with those on the margins, and finding and becoming spiritual companions.

5. *Stepping into the World.* This volume looks at vocation as the divine call to be radically available to God in all we are and all we do. We investigate our own faith stories and gifts, our life's work as vocation, traveling lightly, and seeing life through the eyes of a pilgrim—being sent out into the world with a sense of spiritual purpose.

The Role of Repetition and Liturgy in This Resource

Some leaders who use this resource may wonder why parts of the meeting and selected prayers are repeated week to week. This repeating order of a meeting or service is sometimes called *liturgy*. *Liturgy*, which means "the work of the people," is a powerful tool in prayer. To echo the same words that have been prayed for centuries joins us to Christ and to the saints who have prayed these prayers for generations. Liturgy provides ease in prayer, removing the pressure of coming up with our own words. The liturgy also allows the leader to be a pilgrim alongside younger pilgrims.

One youth leader commented on using this pattern of liturgy in his Wednesday-night youth meetings: "The lives of my kids are crazy and busy, and so is my life! I look forward to an evening when the same structure each week allows me to come and rest in God's presence with the young people. This is the highlight of their week as well. It's not boring; it's a comfort."

Liturgy does not eliminate the need to voice our own personal cries, petitions, and praise to God. Yet in liturgy we find prayers written by people through the ages who have been blessed with the gift of writing beautiful prayers. These prayers are meant to be a catalyst for bringing us into God's holy presence. May they be tools that teach us how to pray and inspire us to find words that echo the prayers of our own hearts and spirits.[1]

The Role of the Leader in Spiritual Formation Groups

Leading a group for spiritual formation differs in many ways from teaching a class. The most obvious difference lies in your basic goal as group leader. In a class, you have particular information (facts, theories, procedures) that you want to convey. You can gauge your success at the end of the class by how well participants demonstrate a grasp of the information.

In a group for spiritual formation, your goal is to enable spiritual growth in each group member. You are working in partnership with the Holy Spirit, who alone can bring about transformation of the human heart. Here, gaining wisdom is more important than gaining knowledge, and growing in holiness is more important than gaining either knowledge or wisdom. Success, if it has any meaning in this context, will be evident over months or even years in the changed lives of group members.

Classes tend to be content-oriented. Groups for spiritual formation tend to be more process-oriented. Even though pilgrims will have completed common preparation in readings and daily exercises, group discussions may move in directions you do not expect. You will need to be open to the movement of the Holy Spirit and vigilant in discerning the difference between following the Spirit's lead and going off on a tangent. Such discernment requires careful, prayerful listening. Listening will be more critical than talking in your role as group leader.

Finally, classes primarily focus on a set of objective data, such as a Bible passage, information in a book, or interpretations of current events. A group for spiritual formation, however, focuses primarily on the personal faith experience of each group member. Each pilgrim is seeking to understand and be open to the grace and revelation of God. Even when group members have read and reflected on a scripture passage, they do not base their discussion on "What did the author intend to say to readers of that time?" but on "How does this passage connect to my life or shed light on my experience?"

Discussion will be a sharing of experience rather than a debate over ideas. You can model this type of personal sharing with your group through your involvement in all parts of the group meeting. Your leadership will differ from that of a traditional youth-group leader or small-group facilitator. You will read the material and complete the daily exercises along with the pilgrims and bring your responses to share with the group. You lead by offering your honest reflections and by trying to enable the young people to listen carefully to one another and to the Spirit in your midst.

Leading a group for spiritual formation requires particular qualities. Foremost among these are patience and trust. You will need patience to let things happen as they happen. Spiritual formation is a lifelong process. It may be difficult to identify any great leaps forward during the months a group will spend on *The Way of Pilgrimage*. It may even take a while for some participants to adjust to the purpose and style of a formational group process.

As a group leader, resolve that when you ask a question, you do not have a "right answer" in mind but really aim for getting participants to talk about their own experience. Setting an example by sharing your experience rather than proclaiming abstract truths or describing the experiences of well-known Christians will foster this shift. Trust that the Holy Spirit will indeed enable pilgrims to see or hear what they need. You may offer what you consider a great insight to which no one responds. If it is what the group needs, though, the Spirit will bring it around again at a more opportune time. Susan Muto, a modern writer on spiritual formation, often says that we need to "make space for the pace of grace." There are no shortcuts to spiritual growth. Be patient and trust the Spirit.

Listening is another critical quality for leading a spiritual formation group. This is not listening for people to say what you hope they will say—so you can jump in and reinforce them. Rather you are listening for what is actually going on. What is happening in pilgrims' minds and hearts may be quite different from what you expect after reading the material and doing the weekly exercises yourself. While you listen, you might want to jot down notes about themes that emerge in the discussion. Does a particular type of experience seem to be at the center of the sharing? Is a particular direction or common understanding emerging—a hint of God's will or a shared sense of something especially beneficial to several members of the group? Is there some action that pilgrims could take together or individually in order to move forward or to respond to a growing sense of call? What do you hear again and again?

A group leader also needs to be accepting. Accept that pilgrims may have had spiritual experiences quite different from yours. Accept that people often see common experiences in different ways. Some may be struck by an aspect that did not impress you at all, while others may be left cold by what truly excites or moves you. As you model acceptance, you will foster acceptance of one another's differences within the group. Besides accepting differences, you will need to accept lack of closure. Group meetings will rarely tie up all the loose ends in a neat package. Burning questions will be left hanging. If important, these questions will surface again (which brings us back to patience and trust). Also be prepared to accept people's emotions along with their thoughts and experiences. Tears, fears, joy, and anger are to be received as legitimate responses along this journey. One expression of acceptance is giving permission. Permit pilgrims to grow and share at their own pace. Let the young people know in the first meeting that while you want to encourage full participation in every part of the process, they are free to "opt out" of anything that makes them feel truly uncomfortable. No one will be forced to share or pray without consent. "Where the Spirit of the Lord is, there is freedom" (2 Cor. 3:17).

In particular, avoid three common tendencies:

1. *Fixing*. When someone presents a specific problem, it will be tempting to find a solution and "fix" the problem. Problem solving generally makes us feel better. Perhaps it makes us feel wise or powerful, or it helps to break the tension; but it will not allow the other person to grow. Moreover, we might prescribe the wrong fix! It is far better, if you have had a similar problem, to speak about your own experience and what worked for you. If you have not had direct experience, perhaps another pilgrim in the group has.

2. *Proselytizing*. You know what has brought you closer to God. Naturally you would like everyone to try it. You can offer your own experience to the group, but trying to convince everyone to follow your path can

be dangerous. Your knowledge and wisdom come into play here. Teresa of Ávila said that if she had to choose between a holy spiritual director and a learned one, she would pick the learned one. The saint might be able to talk only about his or her own spiritual path. The learned one might at least recognize another person's experience from having read about such experiences. It is far more useful to be able to clarify and celebrate another pilgrim's experience of God than to urge others to follow your way.

3. *Controlling*. Many of us are accustomed to filling in silence with some comment. It may be tempting to see ourselves as experts with an appropriate response to whatever anyone says; that is, we tend to dominate and control the conversation. Here again patience and listening are essential. Do not be afraid of silence. Your capacity to be comfortable with silence allows you to be a "nonanxious presence" in the group. If you really cannot bear a long silence, break it with an invitation for someone (maybe a person who has been quiet so far) to share a thought, feeling, or question rather than offer your own comment.

If this style of leadership seems challenging or unfamiliar to you, please seriously consider attending a leader training event for *The Way of Pilgrimage* or Companions in Christ. See www.companionsinchrist.org for training dates and locations. While leadership training is not required for this resource, it is highly recommended and strongly encouraged. Attending this training will give you valuable knowledge and actual practice in leading formationally.

Ground Rules for Group Sharing

By establishing up front some ground rules for group sharing, you may avoid problems. In the Introductory Session, you will be explaining the various components of each week's meeting. It would be good to discuss the nature of sharing times and establish basic rules. Review the following suggestions and add any you wish before presenting them to the group.

- Speak only for yourself about beliefs, feelings, and responses.
- Respect and receive what others offer, even if you disagree.
- Listening is more important than talking. Avoid cross talk—interrupting, speaking for others, or trying to "fix" another person's problems.
- Honor the different ways God works in individuals.

- Don't be afraid of silence. Use it to listen to the Spirit in your midst.
- Maintain confidentiality. What is shared in the group stays in the group.
- Recognize that all group members have permission to share only what and when they are ready to share.

A General Outline for Each Group Meeting

Liturgy of Meeting

The weekly sessions will follow this outline:

Welcoming
Noticing: Listening to Your Life
Moving from Head2Heart
Naming: Reflections on Head2Heart
Blessing and Sending Forth

➤ Welcoming (5 minutes)

Each weekly gathering of the pilgrims provides a respite on the journey. Just as towns, churches, and abbeys welcomed pilgrims in earlier times, welcome the pilgrims into the meeting as a holy space you have created. Before the pilgrims arrive, be attentive to the space: light the candle, have materials prepared and set out, and provide water for refreshment; display anything that communicates in essence: "Welcome! Welcome to this place along the way."

➤ Noticing: Listening to Your Life (10 minutes)

One reason for gathering together weekly as pilgrims on the journey is to assist one another in looking back and taking notice. How was God present to people? And what baggage have pilgrims been carrying around? In this weekly opening exercise, pilgrims will practice looking back through the week. Together they will symbolically leave their "baggage" in a basket (during the time together); then they will name where they noticed God in their week. This exercise encourages being more fully present to God, to one another, and to themselves during the group meeting time.

➤ Moving from Head2Heart (30 minutes)

The intent of this sacred time is to provide space for the message of the daily exercises and readings to move from the mind to the heart—in other words, to move closer to God on this pilgrimage. This segment includes an exercise or practice the group does together. See each weekly gathering for instructions (The How-To) for each Head2Heart exercise.

➤ Naming: Reflections on Head2Heart (15 minutes)

Following the Head2Heart segment comes a time of "naming" in which each pilgrim—alongside companion pilgrims—has the opportunity to articulate and name her or his experience of God through the Head2Heart exercise. Naming is an essential part of the spiritual formation and growth of each pilgrim. Here dots are connected, lightbulbs come on, struggles are affirmed, and journeys intersect.

➤ Blessing and Sending Forth (10 minutes)

Now it's time for the pilgrims to pack their bags, gather what blessings they have received from this holy space, and move out to continue their journey. Sending them forth to continue their journeys is as important as the welcome. The Blessing and Sending Forth should take five to ten minutes.

Concluding Matters

The purpose of the Companions in Christ series (of which *The Way of Pilgrimage* is a part) is to equip persons of faith with both personal and corporate spiritual life practices that will continue long beyond the time frame of this particular resource. Pilgrims may continue certain disciplines on their own and carry some practices into their faith communities. Others may desire the continuation of a small group.

A full Closing Pilgrimage and Retreat model is available for your group at www.companionsinchrist.org/leaders. If you are moving through all five volumes of *The Way of Pilgrimage* consecutively, we suggest you wait till you finish the last volume before leading the retreat. However, the Pilgrimage and Retreat may be used after completion of any of the volumes.

As you guide your group through each six-week journey, you will discover that certain topics generate interest and energy for further exploration. Some pilgrims may wish that they could go into more depth with certain readings or weekly meetings. When the group expresses strong desire to continue with a particular topic or practice, take special note, as this may provide guidance for continued formational exploration beyond *The Way of Pilgrimage*.

Our prayer for you as a leader is that in the weeks ahead you and your group will learn to live as pilgrims in the world and that you will be transformed according to the image of Christ for the sake of the world. May your companionship with Christ and with one another be richly blessed!

INTRODUCTORY SESSION

Use this session as an introductory meeting before you begin your first volume.

Preparation for the Meeting

1. *Prepare yourself spiritually.* Remember as leader that you too are a pilgrim on this journey. The best way to prepare for each gathering is to practice living as a pilgrim yourself. Pray specifically for each pilgrim you journey alongside and for God to be present in your time together just as God is present in places of traditional pilgrimage.

2. *Prepare the space.* The space in which you will rest, pray, and share together on your journey is as sacred as the places of traditional pilgrimage (such as, Notre Dame, the Vatican, or Canterbury). So in some manner claim the space as God's sanctuary by placing in it a candle, cross, piece of fabric, icon, or other symbol to remind the group that you gather in the presence of God and to say to each pilgrim, "Welcome to this holy place."

3. *Prepare the time.* Being familiar with the readings, exercises, prayers, and practices in the Leader's Guide will help the meeting flow more smoothly; you will feel more confident in your guiding; and you will have more freedom to let the Spirit move.

4. *Prepare the materials.* Prepare ahead of time small blank pieces of paper rolled into scrolls (an 8 ½ x 11 sheet of paper cut into equal quarters makes a good size). Also cut an equal number of six- to eight-inch pieces of twine or yarn. These will be used in the Noticing exercise. You will need one scroll for every participant (including yourself) as well as pens and a basket to hold the scrolls. Prepare and post the Ground Rules for Group Sharing from pages 22–23. Also bring an index card for each participant (any size); or you may use disposable luggage tags. Make a copy of the Leader's Guide Preface for each participant. You

will need Bibles for Head2Heart. Post closing body prayer and benediction on page 40 on newsprint or prepare PowerPoint. (Check Blessing and Sending Forth section of your initial volume if not volume 1.)

The Welcoming and the Noticing together comprise the opening prayer of this session. So as much as possible, try to allow them to flow from one to the other. Speaking softly and calmly makes the exercises easier to lead and facilitates the flow of the session. Gentle instrumental music in the background may also be beneficial.

Beginning the Journey

➤ Welcoming (5 minutes)

Remember that each gathering of the pilgrims provides a respite on their journey. Just as towns, churches, and abbeys welcomed pilgrims in earlier times, welcome the pilgrims into the meeting and holy space you have created. Before the pilgrims arrive, be attentive to the space: light the candle, have things set out and prepared, provide water for refreshment; display anything that says, "Welcome! Welcome to this place along the way."

THE HOW-TO

Offer water and talk quietly to the pilgrims as they arrive. Once everyone has arrived and you are ready to begin, say something like:

Welcome. Welcome to this holy place on your journey. It's good to be here. It's good to have you here. Thank you for coming.

Let's begin first by welcoming Christ into our midst and by praying for the time before us.

Opening Prayer

After everyone has been welcomed, allow a little quiet—a holy pause—for people to settle. Invite a pilgrim to light the candle in the center of the room. For this introductory session, use the Opening Prayer from the volume you are about to start (for instance, Volume 1, page 37).

➤ Noticing: Listening to Your Life (10 minutes)

Part of the reason for gathering weekly as pilgrims on the journey is to help each other look back and take notice—of how God was present to us and also of the baggage we have been carrying around with us. In this weekly opening exercise, pilgrims will practice looking back through their week. Together they will leave their "baggage" symbolically in a basket for the duration of the meeting, and then they will name where they noticed God in their week. This exercise will encourage them to be more fully present to God, to one another, and to themselves during the time together.

Let the group members know that in this introductory meeting they will be experiencing all the parts of a regular weekly gathering. Then take time to go over Ground Rules for Group Sharing from this Leader's Guide Introduction. Post these on the wall for all to see as you read through them, or display in PowerPoint. It is a good idea to leave these up for the first several sessions as a visual reminder.

THE HOW-TO

Say something like:

Now we will begin with the Noticing part of our meeting. As we gather together here in this holy space, we want to take a moment and remember where our journeys have taken us this week.

I'd like you to begin by silently looking back through your week, taking special notice of the moments along the way where you felt most alive. When were you most blessed, joyful, or peaceful? We are often able to recognize God's presence through these kinds of moments.

(Pause for reflection.)

We also want to think about what "baggage" we are still carrying from our week. When I say "baggage," I mean all those things that fill up our minds and weigh down our hearts:

> things we are worried about
>
> things we have yet to do or yet to finish
>
> things that left us discouraged
>
> things that have us bouncing off the walls
>
> all those things that distract us in one way or another from being truly present in this place emotionally, mentally, and spiritually.

Let's pray. Close your eyes and settle yourself. Take a few deep breaths and let's practice a holy pause together.

> *(Take a minute or so for this holy pause; you'll know when the pilgrims are settled and ready to engage in the practice of noticing.)*

I invite you, in your own way, to ask Jesus to go with you back to the beginning of the week. Recount your journey day by day through the week. If it helps, imagine yourself walking hand in hand with Jesus, looking at the places, the people, the activities, the interactions, the ups and the downs of your journey this week.

Answer these questions:

> What brought me joy?
> For what am I grateful?
> What weighed me down this week?
> What drained me?
> What worried me or stressed me out?
> When did I feel hope?

(Allow several minutes for the pilgrims to contemplate these questions.)

Now take one of these scrolls of paper, a pen, and a piece of twine. Unroll the scroll, write down the baggage from your week, and then reroll the scroll and tie with the twine. Place your scroll in the basket as an outward sign of inwardly setting aside your baggage so you can enjoy this holy place on your journey and have space to receive what God wants to offer you.

(Allow a few minutes for pilgrims to complete this process.)

Let's share briefly one place on our journey this week where we noticed God through blessing, joy, peace, or any other experience. There may be several instances in your week that you could share, but please keep it to one.

Go around the room allowing each pilgrim, including yourself, to share one experience.

—————

Touching Base on Readings/Exercises

Starting with Week 1 of the volume, you will touch base briefly on the exercises and readings for the week, impressing on the pilgrims the importance of these daily practices for the pilgrimage. They will not have begun using their Participant's Book or journal yet for this introductory meeting.

➤ Head2Heart (30 minutes)

In this gathering, you will invite participants to become pilgrims and to join you on this spiritual journey. Using the Preface and the Introduction in this Leader's Guide, discuss the theology and practice of pilgrimage and what it means to be a pilgrim.

- Pass out copies of the Leader's Guide Preface and read it together. (An abbreviated version of this Preface also appears in the Participant's Book Introduction.)
- Discuss: What is pilgrimage? What is a pilgrim? Why have we forgotten we are pilgrims on a journey? And what is the difference between being a pilgrim and being a tourist?
- Read together Ephesians 3:17-19.
- Discuss how this scripture passage relates to pilgrimage: This is the prayer for our journey. It describes what happens as we travel through this world as pilgrims, as we choose to walk with God and remember who we are.
- Invite the participants to become pilgrims—to walk with God for the next six weeks on this pilgrimage, to open their eyes to the wonder of journeying through this life. We choose to be pilgrims and to make this journey. Becoming a pilgrim is an intentional choice.
- Go over what is asked of the participants as pilgrims on this journey: the daily exercises and readings in the Participant's Book and attending the weekly gatherings. Stress how much richer and more transforming this pilgrimage will be if we all take this commitment seriously together.

Exercise

- Pass out index cards and pens.
- Invite group members to write down a simple expression of their commitment to God for this journey over the next six weeks as an outward sign of their inward commitment to become pilgrims on the way. Let them know this statement will be shared with the group.
- Collect the index cards and read the statements aloud, asking everyone to listen carefully.
- Then together write a collective prayer for the pilgrimage before you as a band of pilgrims.
- Place this prayer in a visible place at each weekly gathering. You might even want to give each pilgrim a copy of it to pray during the week.

The following prayer was created by one *Way of Pilgrimage* test group in Nashville, Tennessee.

God, I will do my best to greet this pilgrimage with open eyes and heart and attempt to use its lessons in my everyday life. I will work to do what I know is right and use this experience to grow closer to you. I commit to keep a godly focus in my prayers and thoughts. Amen.

➤ Naming: Reflections on Head2Heart (15 minutes)

Following the Head2Heart portion is a time of "naming," in which each pilgrim—alongside companion pilgrims—has the opportunity to articulate and name her or his experience of God through the Head2Heart exercise. Naming is an essential part of the spiritual formation and growth of each pilgrim. Here dots are connected, lightbulbs come on, struggles are affirmed, and journeys intersect.

THE HOW-TO

After completing the Head2Heart exercise, ask the following questions, inviting pilgrims to answer as they are comfortable. (In the first few sessions of a volume, you might need to explain what naming is and why it's important.) Other more specific questions might naturally come from the specific exercise.

- **What blessing do you take with you from the exercise we just completed? (That is, what did you learn? What will you take home or carry with you on your journey?)**
- **How did you experience God during the exercise?**
- **Where did you experience the holiness or goodness of God during our gathering today?**
- **How will these experiences of God encourage you on your continued journey?**

➤ Blessing and Sending Forth (10 minutes)

Use the Blessing and Sending Forth from the volume you will begin this week.

Pass out Participant's Books and encourage the pilgrims to begin doing the daily exercises and readings tomorrow for next week's gathering.

VOLUME 1
CHOOSING PILGRIMAGE

Repeating Liturgy for Volume 1

You will use this section each week as you work through this volume. It lists all parts that repeat for every session. Review the materials you need to prepare by turning to the first page of each session under "Preparation for the Meeting."

LITURGY OF MEETING

Welcoming
Noticing: Listening to Your Life
Moving from Head2Heart
Naming: Reflections on Head2Heart
Blessing and Sending Forth

Preparation for the Meeting

1. *Prepare yourself spiritually.* Remember you too are a pilgrim on this journey. The best way to prepare for each gathering is to practice living as a pilgrim yourself. Pray specifically for each pilgrim you journey alongside and for God to be present in your time together just as God is present in places of traditional pilgrimage.

2. *Prepare the space.* The space in which you will rest, pray, and share together on your journey is as sacred as places of traditional pilgrimage (such as Notre Dame, the Vatican, or Canterbury). So claim the space as God's sanctuary by placing in it a candle, cross, piece of fabric, icon, or other symbol to remind the group that you gather in the presence of God and to communicate to each pilgrim, "Welcome to this holy place."

3. *Prepare the time.* Being familiar with the readings, exercises, prayers, and practices in the Leader's Guide will help the meeting flow more smoothly; you will be more more confident in your guiding; and you will have more freedom to let the Spirit move.

4. *Prepare the materials.* Prepare ahead of time small blank pieces of paper rolled up into scrolls (an 8 ½ x 11 sheet of paper cut into equal quarters is a good size). Cut an equal number of six- to eight-inch pieces of twine or yarn for tying scrolls. These will be used in the Noticing exercise. You will need one scroll for every participant (including yourself), pens, and a basket to hold scrolls. You will need Bibles and paper. Post closing body prayer and benediction (page 40) on newsprint or PowerPoint. See each weekly meeting for Head2Heart materials.

—————※※§∞∞∞∞∞————

The Welcoming and the Noticing together comprise the opening prayer of the session. Try to allow the first to flow into the next. Speaking softly and calmly makes leading exercises easier and can facilitate the flow of the session. Gentle instrumental music in the background may also be beneficial.

Remember that each weekly gathering of the pilgrims is a respite on their journey. Just as towns, churches, and abbeys welcomed pilgrims in earlier times, welcome the group's pilgrims into the meeting and holy space you have created. Before the pilgrims arrive, be attentive to the space: light the candle, have materials set out and prepared, provide water for refreshment; include any elements that communicate: "Welcome! Welcome to this place along the way."

➤ Welcoming (5 minutes)

THE HOW-TO

Offer water and talk quietly to the pilgrims as they arrive. Once everyone has arrived and you are ready to begin, say something like:

Welcome. Welcome to this holy place on your journey. It's good to be here. It's good to have you here. Thank you for coming.

Let's begin first by welcoming Christ into our midst and by praying for the time before us.

Lighting the Candle

Once everyone has been welcomed, allow a little quiet (a holy pause) for people to settle. Invite a pilgrim to light the candle in the room. Say:

Leader:	The Lord be with you.
Other Pilgrims:	**And also with you.**

If your group is unfamiliar with this traditional call-and-response, you might introduce it as a way that some more liturgical churches begin prayer. The leader offers a blessing to all present, and the people respond with a blessing for the leader. After the call-and-response, offer the prayer below or one of your choosing.

A PRAYER FOR LIGHT FOR OUR JOURNEY
(Based on Psalm 27 from THE MESSAGE)

Lord Jesus, you are our light. You are our space. Your are our zest. With you we have no need to fear. We gather here in your name asking one thing only: that we might dwell in your presence, contemplate your beauty, and study at your feet. Our hearts whisper to us: "Seek God." And so we come to seek you. Point us down your highway, O God; direct us along well-lit streets. Show us your goodness as we walk this pilgrim's way. Amen.

➤ Noticing: Listening to Your Life (15 minutes)

One reason for gathering together weekly as pilgrims on the journey is to assist one another in looking back and taking notice. How was God present to people? And what baggage have pilgrims been carrying around? In this weekly opening exercise, pilgrims will practice looking back through the week. Together they will symbolically leave their "baggage" in a basket (during the time together); then they will name where they noticed God in their week. This exercise encourages being more fully present to God, to one another, and to themselves during the group meeting time.

THE HOW-TO

Guide participants into this segment:

Now we will begin with the Noticing part of our meeting. As we gather together here in this holy space, we want to take a moment to remember where our journeys have taken us this week.

I'd like you to begin by looking back through your week, taking special notice of the moments along the way when you felt most alive. When were you most blessed, joyful, or peaceful? We are often able to recognize God's presence through these kinds of moments.

(Pause for reflection.)

We also want to think about what "baggage" we are still carrying from our week. When I say "baggage," I mean all those things that fill up our minds and weigh down our hearts:

things we are worried about
things we have yet to do or yet to finish
things that left us discouraged
things that have us bouncing off the walls
all those things that distract us in one way or another from being truly
present in this place emotionally, mentally, and spiritually present.

Let's pray. Close your eyes and settle yourself. Take a few deep breaths and let's practice a holy pause together. (*Take a minute or so for this holy pause; you'll know when the pilgrims are settled and ready to engage in the practice of noticing.*) I invite you, in your own way, to ask Jesus to go with you back to the beginning of this week. Recount your journey day by day through the week. If it helps, imagine yourself walking hand in hand with Jesus, looking at the places, the people, the activities, the interactions, the ups and the downs of your journey this week. Answer these questions:

What brought me joy?
For what am I grateful?
What weighed me down this week?
What drained me?
What worried me?
What stressed me out?
When did I feel hope?

(*Allow several minutes for the pilgrims to contemplate these questions.*)

Now take one of these scrolls of paper, a pen, and a piece of twine. Unroll the scroll, write down the baggage from your week, then reroll the scroll and tie with the twine. Place your scroll in the basket as an outward sign of inwardly setting aside your baggage in order to enjoy this holy place on your journey and have space to receive what God has to offer you.

(*Allow a few minutes for pilgrims to complete this process.*)

Let's share briefly with one place on our journey this week where we noticed God through blessing, joy, peace, or any other experience. There may be several instances in your week that you could share, but please keep it to one.

Go around the room allowing each pilgrim, including yourself, to share one experience.

〰〰〰

Touching Base on Readings/Exercises

What did you notice this past week in the readings and the daily exercises? What do you remember? What stirred you? How did you experience God as you read and practiced the daily exercises?

➤ Moving from Head2Heart (30 minutes)

The intent of this sacred time is to provide space for the message of the daily exercises and readings to move from the mind to the heart—in other words, to move closer to God on this pilgrimage. This segment includes an exercise or practice the group does together. See each weekly gathering for instructions for each Head2Heart exercise.

➤ Naming: Reflections on Head2Heart (15 minutes)

Following the Head2Heart portion comes a time of "naming," in which each pilgrim—alongside companion pilgrims—has the opportunity to articulate and name her or his experience of God through the Head2Heart exercise. Naming is an essential part of the spiritual formation and growth of each pilgrim. Here dots are connected, lightbulbs come on, struggles are affirmed, and journeys intersect.

THE HOW-TO

After completing the Head2Heart exercise, ask the following questions. Have pilgrims answer as they are comfortable. In the first couple of sessions, you might need to explain what naming is and why it's important. Other more specific questions might naturally come from the specific exercise.

- What blessing do you take with you from the exercise we just completed? (That is, what did you learn? What will you take home or carry with you on your journey?)
- How did you experience God during the exercise? Or, how did you experience God's presence?
- How/where did you experience the holiness or goodness of God during our gathering today?
- How will these experiences of God encourage you on your continued journey?

➤ Blessing and Sending Forth (10 minutes)

Now it's time for the pilgrims to pack their bags, gather what blessings they have received from this holy space, and move out to continue their journey. Sending them forth to continue their journeys is as important as the welcome. The Blessing and Sending Forth should take five to ten minutes.

THE HOW-TO

Hand out index cards. Explain that as they prepare to leave and continue their journey, the pilgrims will identify what they have received at this stopping place along the way. Ask them to answer these questions with a word or a phrase:

- What do you need to pack for your pilgrimage?
- What do you need for your journey into this week?

Do this activity quickly. This is not something to think about for a long time. Encourage pilgrims to write the first word or phrase that comes to mind. Then ask them to put their index cards in a back pocket or on the floor in front of them as everyone stands in a circle to pray the body prayer and be sent forth. Once in the circle, pray the following body prayer (post prayer in room or use PowerPoint):

Placing both hands on top of the head, pray out loud:

God be in my head and in my understanding.

Placing both hands over the eyes, pray out loud:

God be in my eyes and in my seeing.

Placing both hands over the ears, pray out loud:

God be in my ears and in my hearing.

Placing both hands over the mouth, pray out loud:

God be in my mouth and in my speaking.

Placing both hands over the heart, pray out loud:

God be in my heart and in my feeling.

Placing both hands on top of the thighs, pray out loud:

God be in my legs and in my moving.

Placing open hands one on top of the other in front of the body, pray out loud:

God be in my hands and in my touching.

Placing both arms at the side of the body, hands open and turning outward, offering our life to God, pray out loud:

God be in my life and in my journeying.[1]

The first time through, have the pilgrims imitate your hand placements and repeat each line of the prayer after you. The second time, pray together.

Send the pilgrims forth into the world to continue their journeys. Use the following dismissal or another blessing. Be as creative as you like.

| **Leader:** | Let us go forth into the world continuing on *The Way of Pilgrimage.* |
| Other Pilgrims: | **Thanks be to God.** |

WEEK 1: Hearing the Call to Pilgrimage

Preparation for the Meeting

1. See page 35 for additional notes about leader preparation and for the basic outline of this session.
2. *Prepare the materials.* In addition to materials listed on page 36, for the Head2Heart portion of the meeting you will need copies of the reflection sheet on Hebrews 12:1-2 for each participant (page 43), pens, journals or extra paper for journaling, and extra Participant's Books for those who weren't present at the introductory session.

You will notice that the Welcoming prayer and Sending Forth prayer are the same for each week in this volume. Repetition and rhythm are essential parts of the spiritual life. Each week we come as pilgrims from the chaos of life to this centering ritual. Help the pilgrims understand that this repetition is purposeful and necessary. As you repeat various elements week after week, you will find that particular prayers, scriptures, and practices begin to sink from your head to your heart, forming you spiritually in the process.

➤ Welcoming (5 minutes)

See page 36 for instructions.

➤ Noticing: Listening to Your Life (15 minutes)

See page 37 for instructions.

➤ Moving from Head2Heart (30 minutes)

THE HOW-TO

Say something like:

The weekly readings remind us that our pilgrimage is both inward and outward, and that the pilgrimage is about being "shaped in the image of Christ by the gracious working of the Holy Spirit for the transformation of the world" (Day 1 Reading).

Today we would like to explore what it means to follow Christ on pilgrimage. What characterizes our lives when we are on pilgrimage? We will take some quiet time now to read and reflect on Hebrews 12:1-2, listening for God's call to our hearts.

Hand out reflection sheets on the Hebrews passage. Point out the journal pages in the back of their Participant's Book, especially for those who have not brought a journal to the meeting. Read the scripture—printed at the top of the reflection sheet on the next page—aloud once.

Now give participants time to review the scripture in silence and complete the reflection sheet. Then ask, **What speaks to you about your pilgrimage in this passage?**

After sharing responses, invite silent prayer for one another.

➤ Naming: Reflections on Head2Heart (15 minutes)

See page 39 for instructions.

➤ Blessing and Sending Forth (10 minutes)

See page 39 for instructions.

REFLECTION SHEET ON HEBREWS 12:1-2

Therefore, since we are surrounded by so great a cloud of witnesses, let us also lay aside every weight and the sin that clings so closely, and let us run with perseverance the race that is set before us, looking to Jesus the pioneer and perfecter of our faith, who for the sake of the joy that was set before him endured the cross, disregarding its shame, and has taken his seat at the right hand of the throne of God.

- Read the passage above slowly and prayerfully, allowing God to address you through it.
- Note in your journal (or in the pages at the back of your Participant's Book) phrases that speak to you about your spiritual journey and where you long to be on that journey.
- Draw a line down the middle of a page in your journal. On the left side, name several "weights" or "sins" that you need to find strength to "lay aside." On the right side, name what you need to "take on" in order to follow Christ as the pioneer of the path you follow.
- Share with God your desire to follow Christ more nearly and for the grace to persevere in that pursuit.

Week 2: A Wilderness Journey

Preparation for the Meeting

1. See page 35 for additional notes about leader preparation and for the basic outline of this session.
2. *Prepare the materials.* In addition to materials listed on page 36, for the Head2Heart portion of the meeting, you will need journals or extra paper for journaling for those who don't have a Participant's Book or journal with them.

Remember that the Welcoming prayer and Sending Forth prayer are the same for each week of this volume. Help the pilgrims understand that this repetition is purposeful and necessary. As you repeat them week after week, you will find that particular prayers, scriptures, and practices begin to sink from your head to your heart, forming you spiritually in the process.

➤ Welcoming (5 minutes)

See page 36 for instructions.

➤ Noticing: Listening to Your Life (15 minutes)

See page 37 for instructions.

➤ Moving from Head2Heart (30 minutes)

THE HOW-TO

The weekly readings tell us the story of Jesus' baptism, a time when he clearly heard the voice of God calling him "beloved." Hearing that same message for ourselves provides the basis for beginning and continuing on the pilgrimage.

Invite your group to listen to the following reading called "Our First Love," by Henri Nouwen, a Roman Catholic priest and great Christian spiritual writer. After the reading, invite people to respond in their journal.

Listen to what God is saying to us:

You are my child.
You are written in the palms of my hand.
You are hidden in the shadow of my hand.

I have molded you in the secret of the earth.
I have knitted you together in your mother's womb.
You belong to me.
I am yours. You are mine.

I have called you from eternity and you are the one who is held safe and embraced in love from eternity to eternity.

You belong to me. And I am holding you safe and I want you to know that whatever happens to you, I am always there. I was always there; I am always there; I always will be there and hold you in my embrace.

You are mine. You are my child. You belong to my home. You belong to my intimate life and I will never let you go. I will be faithful to you.

The spiritual life starts at the place where you can hear God's voice. Where somehow you can claim that long before your father, your mother, your brother, your sister, your school, your church touched you, loved you, and wounded you—long before that, you were held safe in an eternal embrace. You were seen with eyes of perfect love long before you entered into the dark valley of life. . . . The spiritual life starts at the moment that you can go beyond all of the wounds and claim that there was a love that was perfect and unlimited, long before that perfect love became reflected in the imperfect and limited, conditional love of people. The spiritual life starts where you dare to claim the first love—Love one another because I have loved you first.[2]

After reading aloud, ask participants:

What did you hear about your belovedness? What stood out to you? Jot a few words about that in your journal.

Ask participants to keep their journals out for the next exercise. Lead a guided meditation on Mark 1:9-11 with journaling time afterward. Invite participants to get comfortable and to close their eyes. Read the Mark 1:9-11 passage twice. Then invite journaling as you ask the following questions, leaving three to four minutes between each question.

Ponder these questions in your journal.

1. **The world knew Jesus as "Jesus from Nazareth in Galilee." How do people identify you?**

   (time to write)

2. **What do you think it meant to Jesus that God knew him as "my Son, the Beloved; with you I am well pleased"?**

   (time to write)

3. How does God know you? Use your imagination to get into the river of baptism and stand alongside Jesus in the story. Overhear God's blessing as it applies to you, a blessing Jesus wants to share with you. Translate into your own words what this blessing means for you.

(time to write)

Regather and remind participants that they are blessed as individuals and that we as church are a community of blessing and grace. Read story below by Janet Wolf titled "Chosen for. . . ." It emphasizes how we can remind one another of our blessedness in God's eyes.

> In a world that pronounces so many of us "not good enough," what might it mean to believe that we really are chosen, precious, and beloved? In a new members' class we talked about baptism: this holy moment when we are named by God's grace with such power it won't come undone.
>
> Fayette was there—a woman living on the streets, struggling with mental illness and lupus. She loved the part about baptism and would ask over and over, "And when I'm baptized, I am . . . ?" We soon learned to respond, "Beloved, precious child of God and beautiful to behold." "Oh, yes!" she'd say, and then we could go back to our discussion.
>
> The big day came. Fayette went under, came up spluttering, and cried, "And now I am . . . ?" And we all sang, "Beloved, precious child of God and beautiful to behold." "Oh, yes!" she shouted as she danced all around the fellowship hall.
>
> Two months later I got a call. Fayette had been beaten and raped and was at the county hospital. So I went. I could see her from a distance, pacing back and forth. When I got to the door, I heard, "I am beloved . . ." She turned, saw me, and said, "I am beloved, precious child of God, and . . ." Catching sight of herself in the mirror—hair sticking up, blood and tears streaking her face, dress torn, dirty, and rebuttoned askew, she started again, "I am beloved, precious child of God, and . . ." She looked in the mirror again and declared, ". . . and God is still working on me. If you come back tomorrow, I'll be so beautiful I'll take your breath away!"

Offer a prayer: **Lord, baptize us in the waters of your grace that we might remember always who we are and the One to whom we belong. Amen.**[3]

On a table, place a bowl of water and indicate that it represents the waters of baptism. Invite pilgrims to come and together dip their fingers in the water as a reaffirmation of God's blessing and the "grace freely bestowed on us in the Beloved."

Then invite the pilgrims to turn to fellow pilgrims on either side of them (one at a time), take their wet hands, and quietly proclaim God's blessing with words similar to those from the reading:

(Name), you are a beloved, precious child of God and beautiful to behold!

Offer silent prayer for one another.

(An alternative is to have the group say this line in unison for each person in the group. Post the sentence where all can see it.)

➤ Naming: Reflections on Head2Heart (15 minutes)

See page 39 for instructions.

➤ Blessing and Sending Forth (10 minutes)

See page 39 for instructions.

Preparation for the Meeting

1. See page 35 for additional notes about leader preparation and for the basic outline of this session.

2. *Prepare the materials.* In addition to materials listed on page 36, for the Head2Heart portion of the meeting you will need: *It's a Wonderful Life* DVD; DVD player and TV; questions from page 52 preprinted for display in the room; newsprint, chalkboard or dry-erase board with three columns labeled:

> Seeking (Prevenient) Grace
>
> Accepting (Justifying) Grace
>
> Growing (Sanctifying) Grace

Remember to help the pilgrims understand that repetition of the Welcoming and Sending Forth prayers is purposeful. As you repeat them week after week, you will find that particular prayers, scriptures, and practices begin to sink from your head to your heart, forming you spiritually in the process.

➤ Welcoming (5 minutes)

See page 36 for instructions.

➤ Noticing: Listening to Your Life (15 minutes)

See page 37 for instructions.

➤ Moving from Head2Heart (30 minutes)

THE HOW-TO

Reviewing Faces of Grace

The daily exercises and readings about the return of the prodigal son show us a glimpse of the "faces" of the grace of God—seeking us, accepting us, and growing us up—making us more and more like Jesus Christ.

Review briefly the faces of grace described in this week's readings. Display your chosen format with columns labeled "Seeking (Prevenient) Grace," "Accepting (Justifying) Grace," and "Growing (Sanctifying) Grace."

Invite everyone to suggest descriptive words, images, analogies, or Bible stories for each category. Allow participants to look back through their Participant's Book for ideas from this week's daily exercises and readings.

Responding to Stories of Grace (10 minutes)

Read a story of God's amazing grace. Choose either the Augustine or John Wesley account below. Encourage the group to be alert for the faces of grace and for evidence of the means of grace (the ways God draws near to a person), through which God worked in this person's life.

Augustine

I probed the hidden depths of my soul and wrung its pitiful secrets from it, and when I mustered them all before the eyes of my heart, a great storm broke within me, bringing with it a great deluge of tears. I stood up and left Alypius so that I might weep and cry to my heart's content, for it occurred to me that tears were best shed in solitude. I moved away far enough to avoid being embarrassed even by his presence. He must have realized what my feelings were, for I suppose I had said something and he had known from the sound of my voice that I was ready to burst into tears. So I stood up and left him where we had been sitting, utterly bewildered. Somehow I flung myself down beneath a fig tree and gave way to the tears which now streamed from my eyes, the sacrifice that is acceptable to you. I had much to say to you, my God, not in these very words but in this strain: *Lord, will you never be content? Must we always taste your vengeance? Forget the long record of our sins.* For I felt that I was still the captive of my sins, and in my misery I kept crying "How long shall I go on saying 'tomorrow, tomorrow'? Why not now? Why not make an end of my ugly sins at this moment?"

I was asking myself these questions, weeping all the while with the most bitter sorrow in my heart, when all at once I heard the sing-song voice of a child in a nearby house. Whether it was the voice of a boy or a girl I cannot say, but again and again it repeated the refrain "Take it and read, take it and read." At this I looked up, thinking hard whether there was any kind of game in which children used to chant words like these, but I could not remember ever hearing them before. I stemmed my flood of tears and stood up, telling myself that this could only be a divine command to open my book of Scripture and read the first passage on which my eyes should fall. For I had heard the story of Antony, and I remembered how he had happened to go into a church while the Gospel was being read and had taken it as a counsel addressed to himself when he heard the words *Go home and sell all that belongs to you. Give it to the poor, and so the treasure you have shall be in heaven; then come back and follow me.* By this divine pronouncement he had at once been converted to you.

So I hurried back to the place where Alypius was sitting, for when I stood up to move away I had put down the book containing Paul's Epistles. I seized it and opened it, and in silence I read the first passage on which my eyes fell: *Not in revelling and drunkenness, not in lust and wantonness, not in quarrels and rivalries. Rather, arm yourselves with the Lord Jesus Christ; spend no more thought on nature and nature's appetites.* I had no wish to read more and no need to do so. For in an instant, as I came to the end of the sentence, it was as though the light of confidence flooded into my heart and all the darkness of doubt was dispelled.[4]

John Wesley

On May 24, 1738, Wesley received the assurance of faith he had been seeking. The moment was so important to him that he inserted a lengthy spiritual autobiography at this point in his Journal, with eighteen points. This selection picks up at point 12, after Wesley has returned to England from Georgia.

12. When I met Peter Böhler again, he consented to focus the discussion on the issue that I desired, namely, Scripture and experience. I first consulted the Scripture. But when I set aside the glosses of men and simply considered the words of God, comparing them together, endeavoring to illustrate the obscure by the plainer passages, I found they all worked against me. I was forced to retreat to my last hold: that experience would never agree with the literal interpretation of those scriptures, nor could I admit it to be true till I found some living witnesses of it. Accordingly, the next day he came again with three others, all of whom testified of their own personal experience that a true living faith in Christ is inseparable from a sense of pardon for all past—and freedom from all present—sins. They added with one mouth that this faith was the gift, the free gift of God; and that he would surely bestow it upon every soul who earnestly and perseveringly sought it. I was now thoroughly convinced. By the grace of God, I resolved to seek it unto the end: 1. By absolutely renouncing all dependence, in whole or in part, upon my own works or righteousness; on which I had really grounded my hope of salvation, though I did not know it, from my youth up. 2. By adding to the constant use of all the other means of

grace, continual prayer for this very thing—justifying, saving faith, a full reliance on the blood of Christ shed for me, a trust in him, as my Christ, as my sole justification, sanctification, and redemption.

13. I continued thus to seek it (though with strange indifference, dullness, and coldness, and unusually frequent relapses into sin) till Wednesday, May 24. I think it was about five this morning, that I opened my Testament on those words, *He has given us his precious and very great promises, so that through them you may become participants of the divine nature.* Just as I went out, I opened it again on those words, *You are not far from the kingdom of God.* In the afternoon I was asked to go to St. Paul's. The anthem was, *Out of the depths I cry to you, O Lord. Lord, hear my voice! Let your ears be attentive to the voice of my supplications! If you, O Lord, should mark iniquities, Lord, who could stand? But there is forgiveness with you, so that you may be revered. O Israel, hope in the Lord! For with the Lord there is steadfast love, and with him is great power to redeem. It is he who will redeem Israel from all its iniquities.*

14. In the evening I went very unwillingly to a society at Aldersgate Street, where one was reading Luther's preface to the Epistle to the Romans. About a quarter before nine, while he was describing the change that God works in the heart through faith in Christ, I felt my heart strangely warmed. I felt I did trust in Christ, Christ alone for salvation. And an assurance was given me, that he had taken away my sins, even mine, and saved me from the law of sin and death.[5]

After reading, engage in a discussion using these questions:

- **What phrases or images stood out in your mind? What faces of grace did you identify in the story?**
- **What means of grace were involved in the conversion?**
- **Where does the story of Augustine or Wesley connect in some way with your own experience?**
- **What means of grace have played a special role in your journey? How?**

Connecting Our Own Stories with Grace (15 minutes)

After this discussion, show a clip from the movie *It's a Wonderful Life.*[6] Use the entire portion of Frame 11, from 42:27 to 50:10. The clip begins with George Bailey pacing beside the picket fence in front of Mary's house. It ends after the phone call from Sam Wainwright. Referencing the movie, ask participants to think about where they are in their experience of grace:

- Are you walking back and forth by the picket fence, not sure if you are interested in a relationship with God?
- Have you heard someone calling out to you, inviting you to come into the house?
- Are you walking up the sidewalk, trying to decide whether to go in the door?
- Are you sitting uncomfortably and awkwardly in the parlor?
- Are you getting closer?
- Are you "cheek to cheek"?

After reviewing these possibilities, divide into triads and share where you think you are in your experience of God's grace.

➤ Naming: Reflections on Head2Heart (15 minutes)
See page 39 for instructions.

➤ Blessing and Sending Forth (10 minutes)
See page 39 for instructions.

Week 4: The View from the Road

Preparation for the Meeting

1. See page 35 for additional notes about leader preparation and for the basic outline of this session.

2. *Prepare the materials.* In addition to materials listed on page 36, for the Head2Heart portion of the meeting you will need: paper for life pilgrimage maps (varying sizes for preferences), crayons, colored markers, pens and pencils. Either make copies of guiding questions for the life maps or prepare to post on newsprint, dry-erase board, or on PowerPoint.

➤ Welcoming (5 minutes)
See page 36 for instructions.

➤ Noticing: Listening to Your Life (15 minutes)
See page 37 for instructions.

➤ Moving from Head2Heart (30 minutes)

THE HOW-TO

Say something like:

The daily exercises and readings have helped us begin to see the sacredness of our journeys so far—in the places, the people, and time itself. We each have our own sacred story to tell: the story of how God has drawn us near through grace.

We're going to do an exercise about remembering we're on a journey, recognizing that we're pilgrims moving back home toward our God. We are going to draw and write out the map of our pilgrimage through this world thus far.

Exercise

Each of us has traveled our own unique path, and so we each have our own map to draw. You can be as creative as you like with this exercise. You can use crayons or colored markers or pens. You can draw a map, make a time line with dates and words, or write in paragraph form. It doesn't matter how you express this path; it only matters that we practice remembering where we have come from in order to remind ourselves where we are heading. There is no right or wrong way to do this.

Give each pilgrim a copy of the questions on the next page or post them in the room to spark memories of the spiritual journey.

Let participants know that the point of the exercise is not to answer all these questions with their maps; the questions simply provide ideas of what they might include on their maps. Some questions assume church background, and some do not. Have paper, pens, crayons, and colored markers available. Then suggest that pilgrims begin the exercise by taking the materials of their choice and finding a quiet place to sit while mapping their life's pilgrimage. Let them know they will have fifteen to twenty minutes for this exercise.

When participants have finished, gather everyone together with their maps in hand. Allow pilgrims to begin sharing their maps, timelines, or paragraphs and remind them that the group can continue this sharing in next week's session. Take all the time necessary to let each person share. Observe silence between each map story and offer spoken prayer for each person who has shared. Collect the maps before people leave so that they will be on hand for next week.

➤ Naming: Reflections on Head2Heart (10 minutes)

See page 39 for instructions.

➤ Blessing and Sending Forth (10 minutes)

See page 39 for instructions.

LIFE PILGRIMAGE QUESTIONS

- When were you born?

- When were you baptized?

- When do you consider your pilgrimage began?

- When do you first remember learning about God, and what do you remember? Where were you?

- What are your first memories of church or Sunday school?

- Was there a moment when Christ became alive to you?

- When did you commit your life to Christ or offer your heart back to him?

- When did you start to own your faith and believe for yourself?

- When did you come to church because you wanted to, not because you were made to?

- What are some times you have felt closest to God?

- When were you mad at God? Or when did you feel far away from God?

- When was life really hard and you found yourself or those around you struggling?

- What other significant milestones have been a part of your journey?

- Who are your companions on the journey?

- How close are you to God right now? Who is Jesus to you now?

Week 5: Obstacles to Pilgrimage

Preparation for the Meeting

1. See page 35 for additional notes about leader preparation and for the basic outline of this session.

2. *Prepare the materials.* In addition to materials listed on page 36, for the Head2Heart portion of the meeting you will need life pilgrimage maps from last week and access to an indoor or outdoor labyrinth or your church sanctuary.

➤ Welcoming (5 minutes)
See page 36 for instructions.

➤ Noticing: Listening to Your Life (15 minutes)
See page 37 for instructions.

➤ Moving from Head2Heart (30 minutes)

THE HOW-TO

Say something like:

The daily exercises and readings have helped us identify some of the hindrances to the pilgrimage, comparing the journey to climbing a mountain. We discovered that God's grace is present to us all the way up the mountain and back again. Today we will continue sharing our spiritual maps that we began last week.

Take all the time necessary to let each person share. Observe silence between the sharings and speak a prayer for each person who has shared. If you have a small group and finish the maps with plenty of time to spare (or if you finished them last week), you may walk the labyrinth. With a large group, another option is to add a meeting to complete map sharing and/or walk the labyrinth together.

Exercise

An indoor or outdoor labyrinth is best for this exercise. But if you do not have access to a labyrinth, use the sanctuary of your church.

Say something like:

One aspect of setting forth on a pilgrimage involves leaving things behind. Medieval pilgrims took care of all unsettled business before setting forth. They apologized to those they had wronged so that they could move on fully engaged in the pilgrimage before them. We, too, have things we need to leave behind—things that hinder us—in order to make more room for God and the path of life God sets before us. So we look at what habits or things we would do well to leave behind and what holy habits we might practice to help us be more aware of the presence of God that draws us onward.

The labyrinth symbolizes pilgrimage. When medieval pilgrims were not able to make a pilgrimage to the Holy Land, they walked labyrinths instead. Classically three stages of walking the labyrinth are described:

1. *Purgation (Releasing)*: As you enter the labyrinth, you release or let go of the details of your life. This act of shedding thoughts and distractions allows a time to open the heart and quiet the mind.

2. *Illumination (Receiving)*: Reaching the center—where you can stay as long as you like—you are in a place of meditation and prayer. You receive what is there for you to receive.

3. *Union (Returning)*: As you leave, following the same path out from the center that you walked in on, you enter the third stage, which is joining God at work in the world.[7]

Today we will create our own pilgrimage, reflecting on what we need to lay aside and what we need to take on as we journey forward. As we walk this labyrinth together, we will consider these questions:

- On the way in to the center: *What do I need to let go of in my life?*
- On the way out from the center: *What do I need to put on or take up for the pilgrimage?*

If you use the sanctuary for your pilgrimage, have everyone start by standing at the back of the sanctuary. Say: **Consider these pews as your pilgrimage road, your own prayer path. In silence wander down and back, in and among the pews making your way to the altar. As you walk, consider the** question: What do I need to let go of—attitudes, habits, things—to make room for God in my life?

When you get to the altar, take whatever time you need to rest in God's presence. When you are ready to return, walk back through the rows of pews and ask yourself this question: What holy habits do I need to take up in order to join God at work in this world?

Gather back at your designated place for the Naming portion of the meeting.

➤ Naming: Reflections on Head2Heart (15 minutes)
See page 39 for instructions.

➤ Blessing and Sending Forth (10 minutes)
See page 39 for instructions.

Week 6: Outfitted for Pilgrimage

Preparation for the Meeting

1. See page 35 for additional notes about leader preparation and for the basic outline of this session.
2. *Prepare the materials.* In addition to materials listed on page 36, for the Head2Heart portion of the meeting you will need: road sign categories posted on newsprint, poster board or large construction paper, markers, crayons, scissors, glue, and pencils or pens, enough *Way of Pilgrimage* Volume 2 Participant's Books for each participant (to pass out at the end of meeting).

➤ Welcoming (5 minutes)

See page 36 for instructions.

➤ Noticing: Listening to Your Life (15 minutes)

See page 37 for instructions.

➤ Moving from Head2Heart (30 minutes)

Say something like:

The daily exercises and readings have helped us identify some of the ways we are "outfitted" for pilgrimage. While last week we focused on what we needed to cast off—the hindrances and obstacles—this week we focus on what we want to put on, like humility, worship, patience, and trust. Today we will work on some "rules for the road" that help us to be outfitted for the pilgrimage.

In this session we also will look back on the five weeks we've spent together so far—a wrap-up and review.

THE HOW-TO

Exercise

Say something like:

Once the pilgrim heart has awakened, life changes. Once you're a pilgrim, you're always a pilgrim—there is no turning back. Being a pilgrim becomes the lens through which you see the world and yourself. We are a pilgrim people. As T. S. Eliot wrote in "Little Gidding," after we make our journeys we arrive back at the beginning "and know the place for the first time."[8] How is life different? How are you different? How do you see things differently?

Reflect together over the past five meetings. You might want to review briefly what each meeting covered.

NOTES FOR REVIEW

Introductory session: Writing expressions of commitment; creating a collective prayer together

Week 1: Talking about Jesus, the pioneer of our faith (Hebrews 12:1-2)

Week 2: Experiencing guided meditation on Mark 1:9-11; remembering our baptism: "*(Name)*, you are beloved, precious child of God and beautiful to behold!"

Week 3: Listening for grace in stories of Augustine or John Wesley and in a scene from *It's a Wonderful Life*

Week 4: Drawing spiritual maps

Week 5: Sharing spiritual maps; meditative walking (labyrinth or sanctuary)

Ask: **What sticks out in your mind? What group exercises do you remember?** Encourage pilgrims especially to remember what it was they desired or were seeking at the beginning of these six weeks together.

Next invite pilgrims to develop their own "rules for the road"—things they need to remember; warnings and hazards; practices they need to continue; behaviors, attitudes, or ideas to leave on the side of the road.

Rules for the road help us keep to the path where God is leading and provide tools for remembering we are pilgrims who seek our way home to God.

Remind participants that the journey does not end here; rather, here and now their journey begins once again. Begin by reviewing some of the expressions of commitment that your group developed together in the introductory session (see pages 29–34 in this Leader's Guide). Post these commitments again where all can see if they are not already posted.

Discuss this question: **How have we done with these commitments so far?**

Say: **We are on a journey together as a community in Christ. We are one-fifth of the way through** *The Way of Pilgrimage.* **What are the most important rules for the road as pilgrims? Which rules for the road do we want to remind ourselves and other pilgrims about?**

Making "Rules for the Road" Signs

We are going to make signs today to remind ourselves and other pilgrims of rules that keep our hearts and minds focused on Christ.

Provide materials for the pilgrims to create the signs. Post these categories to prompt their creativity:

- Road signs (Yield, Stop, One Way, etc.)
- Historical Markers
- Rest Areas
- Celebrations
- Gas and Food
- Exit and Entrances

Give people time to work on their signs. Encourage them to think about what lies behind the meaning of their signs and to jot notes on the back of each sign they create.

When pilgrims have finished designing their road signs, ask them to share with the group. Then have people hold out their signs faceup on their palms. Offer a prayer, dedicating the rules for the road and these paths to God. Ask in prayer that all may be faithful on the pilgrimage. Conclude with **Thanks be to God. Amen.**

➤ Naming: Reflections on Head2Heart (15 minutes)

See page 39 for instructions.

➤ Blessing and Sending Forth (10 minutes)

See page 39 for instructions.

NOTE: Make sure the pilgrims know about your plans to continue with Volume 2, *The Bible: Pilgrimage Travel Guide.* If you are starting that volume next week, have the new Participant's Books on hand for distribution at the conclusion of this meeting.

If you want to have a pilgrimage retreat after this volume, you can find a retreat model at www.companionsinchrist.org/leaders.

VOLUME 2
THE BIBLE: PILGRIMAGE TRAVEL GUIDE

Repeating Liturgy for Volume 2

You will use this section each week as you work through this volume. It lists all parts that repeat for every session. Review the materials you need to prepare by turning to the first page of each session under "Preparation for the Meeting."

LITURGY OF MEETING

Welcoming
Noticing: Listening to Your Life
Moving from Head2Heart
Naming: Reflections on Head2Heart
Blessing and Sending Forth

Preparation for the Meeting

1. *Prepare yourself spiritually.* Remember you too are a pilgrim on this journey. The best way to prepare for each gathering is to practice living as a pilgrim yourself. Pray specifically for each pilgrim you journey alongside and for God to be present in your time together just as God is present in places of traditional pilgrimage.

2. *Prepare the space.* The space in which you will rest, pray, and share together on your journey is as sacred as places of traditional pilgrimage (such as Notre Dame, the Vatican, or Canterbury). So claim the space as God's sanctuary by placing in it a candle, cross, piece of fabric, icon, or other symbol to remind the group that you gather in the presence of God and to communicate to each pilgrim, "Welcome to this holy place."

3. *Prepare the time.* Being familiar with the readings, exercises, prayers, and practices in the Leader's Guide will help the meeting flow more smoothly; you will be more more confident in your guiding; and you will have more freedom to let the Spirit move.

4. *Prepare the materials.* Prepare ahead of time small blank pieces of paper rolled up into scrolls (an 8 ½ x 11 sheet of paper cut into equal quarters is a good size). Cut an equal number of six- to eight-inch pieces of twine or yarn for tying scrolls. These will be used in the Noticing exercise. You will need one scroll for every participant (including yourself), pens, and a basket to hold the scrolls. You will need Bibles and paper. Post closing body prayer and benediction on newsprint or PowerPoint. See each weekly meeting for necessary Head2Heart materials.

〰〰〰

The Welcoming and the Noticing together comprise the opening prayer of the session. So as much as possible (especially as pilgrims become familiar with the pattern of the meeting and with the exercises themselves) try to allow the first to flow into the next. Speaking softly and calmly makes leading exercises easier and can facilitate the flow of the session. Gentle instrumental music in the background may also be beneficial.

Remember that each weekly gathering of the pilgrims is a respite on their journey. Just as towns, churches, and abbeys welcomed pilgrims in earlier times, welcome the group's pilgrims into the meeting and holy space you have created. Before the pilgrims arrive, be attentive to the space: light the candle, have materials set out and prepared, provide water for refreshment; include any elements that communicate: "Welcome! Welcome to this place along the way."

➤ Welcoming (5 minutes)

THE HOW-TO

Offer water and talk quietly to the pilgrims as they arrive. Once everyone has arrived and you are ready to begin, say something like:

Welcome. Welcome to this holy place on your journey. It's good to be here. It's good to have you here. Thank you for coming.

Let's begin first by welcoming Christ into our midst and by praying for the time before us.

Lighting the Candle

Once everyone has been welcomed, allow a little quiet (a holy pause) for people to settle. Invite a pilgrim to light the candle in the room. Say:

Leader: The Lord be with you.

Other Pilgrims: **And also with you.**

If your group is unfamiliar with this traditional call-and-response, you might introduce it as a way that some more liturgical churches begin prayer. The leader offers a blessing to all present, and the people respond with a blessing for the leader. After the call-and-response, offer the prayer below or one of your choosing.

A Prayer for Light for Our Journey
(Based on Psalm 119, The Message)

Through your word, O Lord, I can see where I am going; your word throws a beam of light on my dark path. Bless us, Lord Jesus, our guide on this journey. Bless us and keep us on course. Help us to walk steadily on the road you have revealed for each of us, knowing that we are blessed when we follow your directions. Lord Jesus, our light and our lamp, as we gather together on our journey, let us find you. Amen.

➤ Noticing: Listening to Your Life (15 minutes)

Part of the reason for gathering weekly as pilgrims on the journey is to help one another look back and take notice—of how God was present to us and also of the baggage we have been carrying around with us. In this weekly opening exercise, pilgrims will practice looking back through their week. Together they will leave their baggage symbolically in a basket for the time together and then they will name where they noticed God in their week. This exercise will help them to be more fully present to God, to one another, and to themselves during the time together.

THE HOW-TO

Offer these instructions:

Now we will begin with the Noticing part of our meeting. As we gather together here in this holy space, we want to take a moment and remember where our journeys have taken us this week.

I'd like you to begin by looking back through your week, taking special notice of the moments along the way where you felt most alive. When were you most blessed, joyful, or peaceful? We are often able to recognize God's presence through these kinds of moments.

(Pause for reflection.)

We also want to think about what "baggage" we are still carrying from our week. When I say "baggage," I mean all those things that fill up our minds and weigh down our hearts:

> things we are worried about
>
> things we have yet to do or yet to finish
>
> things that left us discouraged
>
> things that have us bouncing off the walls
>
> all those things that distract us in one way or another from being present in this place (not physically present—clearly, you're here—but emotionally, mentally, and spiritually present).

Let's pray. Close your eyes and settle yourself. Take a few deep breaths and let's practice a holy pause together.

(Take a minute or so for this holy pause; you'll know when the pilgrims are settled and ready to engage in the practice of noticing.)

I invite you, in your own way, to ask Jesus to go with you back to the beginning of the week. Recount your journey day by day through the week. If it helps, imagine yourself walking hand in hand with Jesus, looking at the places, the people, the activities, the interactions, the ups and the downs of your journey this week. Answer these questions:

> What brought me joy?
>
> For what am I grateful?
>
> What weighed me down this week?
>
> What drained me?
>
> What worried me?
>
> What stressed me out?

(Allow several minutes for the pilgrims to contemplate these questions.)

Now take one of these scrolls of paper, a pen, and a piece of twine. Unroll the scroll, write down the baggage from your week, and then reroll the scroll and tie with the twine. Place your scroll in the basket as an outward sign of inwardly setting aside your baggage in order to enjoy this holy place on your journey and have space to receive what God has to offer you.

(Allow a few minutes for pilgrims to complete this process.)

Let's share briefly one place on our journey this week where we noticed God through blessing, joy, peace, or any other experience. There may be several instances in your week that you could share, but please keep it to one.

Go around the room allowing each pilgrim, including yourself, to share one experience

—≈≈≈≈≈≈—

Touching Base on Readings/Exercises

What did you notice this past week in the readings and the daily exercises? What do you remember? What stirred you? How did you experience God as you read and practiced the daily exercises?

➤ Moving from Head2Heart (30 minutes)

The intent of this sacred time is to provide space for the message of the daily exercises and readings to move from the mind to the heart—in other words, to move closer to God on this pilgrimage. This segment includes an exercise or practice the group does together. See each weekly gathering for instructions for specific Head2Heart exercises.

➤ Naming: Reflections on Head2Heart (15 minutes)

Following the Head2Heart portion comes a time of "naming," in which each pilgrim—alongside companion pilgrims—has the opportunity to articulate and name her or his experience of God through the Head2Heart exercise. Naming is an essential part of the spiritual formation and growth of each pilgrim. Here dots are connected, lightbulbs come on, struggles are affirmed, and journeys intersect.

THE HOW-TO

After completing the Head2Heart exercise, ask the following questions. Let pilgrims answer as they are comfortable. (In the first few sessions in a volume, you might need to explain what "naming" is and why it's important.) Other more specific questions might naturally arise from the particular exercise.

- What blessing do you take with you from the exercise we just completed? (That is, what did you learn? What will you take home or carry with you on your journey?)
- How did you experience God during the exercise?
- How/where did you experience the holiness or goodness of God during our gathering today?
- How will these experiences of God encourage you on your continued journey?

➤ Blessing and Sending Forth (10 minutes)

Now it's time for the pilgrims to pack their bags, gather what blessings they have received from this holy space, and move out to continue their journey. Sending them forth to continue their journeys is as important as the welcome. The Blessing and Sending Forth should take five to ten minutes.

THE HOW-TO

Copy for each person or post the closing prayer and benediction so that everyone can pray together.

Hand out index cards and pens. Tell the pilgrims that as they prepare to leave and continue their journey, they must first gather what they have received from this place along the way. Say something like:

What have you heard during this gathering? Can you put that thought into a word or phrase that you have received from God?

Explain that they may have a clear word or phrase; they may sense God has taught them something; or they may have felt an assurance of some sort. The more the pilgrims practice this exercise, the easier it will become.

As we prepare to leave, I invite you to write down a word or phrase expressing what you may have heard from God during this time. Now fold up the card and place it in your pocket or Bible as a reminder that God's Word continues to walk with you on the journey beyond this gathering and that God has spoken to you in this place. By putting it in your pocket you literally take God's Word into our world. It reminds you to continue listening for God.

Gather the band of pilgrims in a circle together holding hands. Pray this closing prayer:

Jesus, you are the Word made flesh. As we hold in our pockets the word you have spoken to each of us, may we continue to listen for your voice through this week. And may your word continue to guide us in our pilgrimage through life. Amen.

Send the pilgrims forth into the world to continue their journeys using the following dismissal or another blessing. Be as creative as you like.

Leader: Let us go forth into the world continuing on *The Way of Pilgrimage.*

Other Pilgrims: **Thanks be to God.**

Week 1: The Living, Breathing Word of God

Preparation for the Meeting

1. See page 63 for additional notes about leader preparation and for the basic outline of this session.

2. *Prepare the materials.* In addition to materials listed on page 64, for the Head2Heart portion of the meeting you will need: Bibles, concordances, commentaries, Bible dictionaries, journals, extra paper, pens, the Informational / Formational signs to post at front of room, index cards prepared with one statement on each card from Informational Reading/ Formational Reading chart on page 72, questions for Head2Heart posted on newsprint or PowerPoint, copies of the Reflection Sheet on Formational Reading (page 73) for each person.

Note: The Naming portion for this session differs from the repeating liturgy found on page 67.

You will notice that the Welcoming prayer and Sending Forth prayer are the same for each week in this volume. Repetition and rhythm are essential parts of the spiritual life. Each week we come as pilgrims from the chaos of life to this centering ritual. Help the pilgrims understand that this repetition is purposeful and necessary. As you repeat various elements week after week, you will find that particular prayers, scriptures, and practices begin to sink from your head to your heart, forming you spiritually in the process.

➤ Welcoming (5 minutes)

See page 64 for instructions.

➤ Noticing: Listening to Your Life (15 minutes)

See page 65 for instructions.

➤ Moving from Head2Heart (30 minutes)

THE HOW-TO

Say something like:

Reading for information is an integral part of teaching and learning. But reading also involves listening for special guidance, a particular insight—for growing your relationship with God. What matters is the attitude of the mind and heart.

Exercise

Post signs with the words "INFORMATIONAL" and "FORMATIONAL" at the front of the room. Pass out sentences describing the two types of reading (found on page 72) on index cards. Give the group time to arrange the cards under the proper headings. Discuss the similarities and differences.

Explain that everyone will now have time to explore one passage of scripture in both an informational and a formational way. Provide enough concordances, commentaries, and Bible dictionaries so everyone in the group has at least one reference book. Give them time to spread out, read Luke 4:14-22, and answer the following questions in their journals (read these aloud and post them also):

1. What did you learn that is interesting to you?
2. How do the facts help you understand the passage differently or better?
3. What do you think Luke wanted readers to understand about Jesus and his call to discipleship through this story?

After about fifteen minutes hand out the Reflection Sheet on Formational Reading. Give people fifteen minutes for solitary reflection.

For Index Cards: Write each statement below on a separate index card for use in the first Head2Heart exercise. Do not indicate on the card which category the sentence falls under.

[INFORMATIONAL READING]

- Covers as much material as possible as quickly as possible

- Seeks an objective meaning, truth, or principle to apply

- Seeks to master the text as an object to control

- Analytical and critical

- Concerned with solving a problem

[FORMATIONAL READING]

- Covers small portions of content and savors slowly

- Focuses on depth; seeks multiple layers of meaning in a single passage

- Allows the text to master the student as an object to be shaped by the text

- Requires a humble, willing, loving approach to the text

- Open to mystery

REFLECTION SHEET ON FORMATIONAL READING

The most basic question we bring to our reading of scripture is: **What is God calling us to do and be?**

Reread Luke 4:14-22. Try not to read it as a Christian in the twenty-first century. Hear Jesus' words as a member of the body of Christ that is universal and present in all time.

1. Select the phrase you hear most clearly or that seems to claim you. Spend a few minutes exploring its meaning for you. Why did it draw your attention?

2. Consider ways you could enact or embody this word—today, tomorrow, or this week. Share your thoughts with God. Write them here:

3. As a member of the body of Christ, complete this sentence:
   The Spirit of the Lord is upon me, because he has anointed me to . . .

Give thanks to God for the particular way God is inviting you to share in Christ's life.

➤ Naming: Reflections on Head2Heart (15 minutes)

See page 67 for instructions. For this session, offer an opportunity to debrief the preceding exercise as follows.

Gather the group to share reflections on the passage. Invite all members to share their responses to the final question on the reflection sheet: "The Spirit of the Lord is upon me, because he has anointed me to _____."

Ask the group to discuss what they learned about the two approaches to scripture. You might use the following questions:

1. How is this approach to scripture similar or different from the way you usually read scripture?
2. How would you describe the differences between the information and formational readings?
3. What have you learned that would help you enter more deeply into scripture?[1]

➤ Blessing and Sending Forth (10 minutes)

See page 68 for instructions.

Week 2: Our Story: The Good, the Bad, and the Family

Preparation for the Meeting

1. See page 63 for additional notes about leader preparation and for the basic outline of this session.
2. *Prepare the materials.* In addition to materials listed on page 64, for the Head2Heart portion of the meeting you will need: copies of Reflection Sheet on Psalm 119:1-12 (page 77) for each participant, pens, journals and extra paper, journaling questions (page 76) posted on newsprint or PowerPoint.

Remember that the Welcoming prayer and Sending Forth prayer are the same for each week of this volume. Help the pilgrims understand that this repetition is purposeful and necessary. As you repeat them week after week, you will find that particular prayers, scriptures, and practices begin to sink from your head to your heart, forming you spiritually in the process.

➤ Welcoming (5 minutes)
See page 64 for instructions.

➤ Noticing: Listening to Your Life (15 minutes)
See page 65 for instructions.

➤ Moving from Head2Heart (30 minutes)

THE HOW-TO

Say something like:

As we journey together we are exploring and discovering the Bible as a travel guide. The Bible for Christians is a memory album, full of pictures and stories from our family history. When we open the Bible, we find our family stories (like Abraham, Moses, Mary, Jesus, and Peter), poems by family members (the Psalms), dreams and visions for our family (Isaiah, Daniel, Revelation), wisdom for daily life (Proverbs, Jesus' parables), and even grandfatherly advice (Paul's letters). By knowing our stories we get a better understanding of who we are. By identifying with our stories we are able to live our lives more faithfully as God's pilgrim people.

Last week, we discussed the difference between informational and formational approaches to scripture. One formational approach is "spiritual reading." Let's explore what is involved in spiritual reading and then practice it.

Exercise

Ask the members of your group to think about the differences between reading the newspaper and reading a personal letter, or between reading a car manual and reading the Bible. Direct the group to form four groups. Assign each group one category—newspaper, letter, car manual, Bible—and answer the following questions (you can read these aloud):

- **Why would you read this?**
- **When would you read it?**
- **What kind of information would you get?**
- **How would you read it—fast, slow, skimming, or thoroughly?**

Ask the newspaper and car manual groups to share their responses, followed by the other two groups. Discuss the differences. Point out that spiritual reading is more like reading a personal letter. Then direct pilgrims to find a comfortable space with their journals and Bibles. Explain:

I'm going to read aloud Psalm 119:1-12. As you listen, pay attention to your feelings.

After you read the passage, ask people to journal their responses to the following questions (may be posted on newsprint or PowerPoint):

- How do I feel about what is being said? What is my gut reaction?
- Why do I feel this way? Where do these feelings come from?
- What is going on inside me?

After allowing time for participants to journal, invite them to share their insights with one other person in the group. Pass out copies of the Reflection Sheet on Psalm 119:1-12. Then say:

Now read the scripture by yourself, taking your own time. Respond on the reflection sheet.

REFLECTION SHEET ON PSALM 119:1-12

Happy are those whose way is blameless,
    who walk in the law of the LORD.
Happy are those who keep his decrees,
    who seek him with their whole heart,
who also do no wrong,
    but walk in his ways.
You have commanded your precepts
    to be kept diligently.
O that my ways may be steadfast
    in keeping your statutes!
Then I shall not be put to shame,
    having my eyes fixed on all your commandments.
I will praise you with an upright heart,
    when I learn your righteous ordinances.
I will observe your statutes;
    do not utterly forsake me.

How can young people keep their way pure?
    By guarding it according to your word.
With my whole heart I seek you;
    do not let me stray from your commandments.
I treasure your word in my heart,
    so that I may not sin against you.

1. How do I treasure God's Word in my heart?

2. In what aspects of scripture do I delight? What is God saying to me
   in these verses?

➤ Naming: Reflections on Head2Heart (15 minutes)

See page 67 for instructions.

➤ Blessing and Sending Forth (10 minutes)

See page 68 for instructions.

Week 3: Shaped by the Word on Pilgrimage

Preparation for the Meeting

1. See page 63 for additional notes about leader preparation and for the basic outline of this session.
2. *Prepare the materials.* In addition to materials listed on page 64, for the Head2Heart portion of the meeting, you will need: Bibles, *Big Fish* DVD, DVD player and TV, journals, pens, extra paper.

Remember to help the pilgrims understand that repetition of the Welcoming and Sending Forth prayers is purposeful. As you repeat them week after week, you will find that particular prayers, scriptures, and practices begin to sink from your head to your heart, forming you spiritually in the process.

➤ Welcoming (5 minutes)
See page 64 for instructions.

➤ Noticing: Listening to Your Life (15 minutes)
See page 65 for instructions.

➤ Moving from Head2Heart (30 minutes)

THE HOW-TO

Say something like:

Sometimes the stories of the Bible seem too fantastic to be true—a burning bush that is not consumed, a man living in the belly of a whale, or Jesus feeding five thousand people with just five loaves of bread and two fish. Even more outrageous is the unconditional love and abounding grace that God offers to us through Jesus Christ. We have story after fantastic story that recount and affirm God's continuous efforts to reach out, draw us in, and walk with us on this journey of faith. These are not just ancient stories and adventures of the distant past. These are our stories; they serve as the introduction to the chapters we are writing with our own lives.

Exercise: Hearing Our Story

Part 1: _LECTIO_

1. Invite the group to spend a few moments paying attention to their breathing and becoming still.

2. Ask pilgrims to listen for a word or phrase that stands out to them as you read Mark 6:35-44. Read the passage slowly. Instruct them that when they have their word or phrase, they should continue to say that word or phrase to themselves slowly, letting it sink into their mind and heart.

3. Read Mark 6:35-44 again slowly. Then allow some time for reflection. Invite pilgrims to let connections, memories, and images surface.

4. Read the passage a third time. Invite pilgrims to pray to God about the word or phrase and what it might mean for their life.

5. Invite everyone to share aloud their prayer word or phrase without elaborating on its meaning for them.

Part 2: LIVING THE WORD

1. Watch a movie clip from _Big Fish_ described in Reading 3 of the Participant's Book. (In this section young William Bloom is in bed with chicken pox. His father recounts a three-year stint in bed and what happened after those three years.)

2. Discuss this clip using the following discussion starters:

- **Why is Edward telling these stories? What is their value?**
- **Why is William frustrated?**
- **Are the stories less valuable if they did not actually happen?**

3. Give participants time to think about and write down Bible stories they wonder about. Then invite them to ponder these questions:

- **What is the value or message in the story?**
- **Does the message change if you have doubts about whether the events really happened?**

After five minutes, invite them to share responses with the group.

4. If time allows, discuss how these ancient stories are relevant today.

➤ Naming: Reflections on Head2Heart (15 minutes)

See page 67 for instructions.

➤ Blessing and Sending Forth (10 minutes)

See page 68 for instructions.

Week 4: Walking with the Word

Preparation for the Meeting

1. See page 63 for additional notes about leader preparation and for the basic outline of this session.
2. *Prepare the materials.* In addition to materials listed on page 64, for the Head2Heart portion of the meeting, you will need: a large enough space to do "sculpting" exercise, your own Bible, and a pencil.

➤ Welcoming (5 minutes)

See page 64 for instructions.

➤ Noticing: Listening to Your Life (15 minutes)

See page 65 for instructions.

➤ Moving from Head2Heart (30 minutes)

THE HOW-TO

Exercise

Part 1: *LECTIO*

1. Invite the group to spend a few moments paying attention to their breathing and becoming still.

2. Ask pilgrims to listen for a word or phrase that stands out to them as you read Ezekiel 37:1-10. Read the passage slowly. Explain that when they have their word or phrase, they can say that word or phrase to themselves slowly, letting it sink into their mind and heart.

3. Read Ezekiel 37:1-10 again slowly. After you have read through the passage the second time, allow some time for reflection on connections, images, and meanings.

4. Then read the passage again. Invite pilgrims to pray to God about the word or phrase and what it might mean for their life.

5. Invite everyone to share their prayer word or phrase aloud without elaboration.

As leader, note down the words or phrases spoken and mark them in your Bible with a pencil.

Part 2: LIVING THE WORD

Say something like:

Just as we can meditate alone, we can also meditate together. In the process of meditation, the words of scripture can shape and sculpt us—individually and as a community.

Ask for a volunteer to be a "sculptor" and three or four people to be "sculpted." Encourage the group to maintain stillness and an attitude of prayer while meditating on the sculpted images that will be formed in front of them.

Read the Ezekiel passage one more time, pausing at the words or phrases that people named in Part 1. During the pauses, have the sculptor arrange the rest of the group into a human sculpture that illustrates that word or idea. Leave a minute for everyone to absorb and appreciate the body sculpture before continuing to read the text.

➤ Naming: Reflections on Head2Heart (15 minutes)

See page 67 for instructions.

➤ Blessing and Sending Forth (10 minutes)

See page 68 for instructions.

Week 5: Allowing the Word to Shape Our Imagination

Preparation for the Meeting

1. See page 63 for additional notes about leader preparation and for the basic outline of this session.
2. *Prepare the materials.* In addition to materials listed on page 64, for the Head2Heart portion of the meeting, you will need: journals and extra paper.

Note: The Naming portion of this session differs from the repeating liturgy found on page 67. See page 85.

➤ Welcoming (5 minutes)
See page 64 for instructions.

➤ Noticing: Listening to Your Life (15 minutes)
See page 65 for instructions.

➤ Moving from Head2Heart (10 minutes)

THE HOW-TO

Say something like:

Different people find different approaches to prayer suited to them. The imagination exercises this week may have been difficult or uncomfortable, but they might have pushed you to use mental and spiritual "muscles" that you rarely employ. By using the imagination, we carry on a conversation with biblical figures and events through which God chose to speak. We try to become part of the story, picturing it and identifying with the persons described. As we enter into the story this way, it can open up insight, inspire us, and enliven us.

Lead the group in a guided imagery meditation based on John 8:2-11.

• First, read the Gospel story aloud and invite participants to list the images that are most vivid for them.

• Then prepare the group for a meditation based on this story by asking everyone to listen with eyes closed and to free their imaginations to see, hear, feel, smell, make associations, and participate in the story. Encourage them to keep their journals ready for jotting down discoveries or insights.

• Invite a moment of silence and prayer using words like these: **God, reveal your grace and truth through the gift of creative imagination you have given each of us.**

• Lead the group in the following guided imagery meditation. Remember to read slowly. Pause for about fifteen seconds at the ellipses (. . .) between questions so participants have time to let questions sink in and reflect on them.

Early in the morning he came again to the temple. All the people came to him and he sat down and began to teach them.

Visualize the scene. Imagine Jesus coming to the Temple with his disciples, as was his custom day after day. Imagine people gathering about, sitting down around him, as he begins to teach. What do you see? . . . What does it feel like to be here? . . . Why are you here?

The scribes and the Pharisees brought a woman who had been caught in adultery; and making her stand before all of them, they said to him, "Teacher, this woman was caught in the very act of committing adultery."

Identify with the woman. Who are you, and what is your life like? . . . How do you feel as you are brought before Jesus and made to stand before all these men? . . . How do you feel about your accusers? . . . How does Jesus look at you as they bring you forward? . . .

They said to him, "Teacher, this woman was caught in the very act of committing adultery. Now in the law Moses commanded us to stone such women. Now what do you say?" They said this to test him, so that they might have some charge to bring against him.

Identify with one of the scribes or Pharisees. How do you feel about what you are doing right now? . . . How do you feel about this woman? . . . How does Jesus look at you as you bring her forward and make your charges?

Jesus bent down and wrote with his finger on the ground. When they kept on questioning him, he straightened up and said to them, "Let anyone among you who is without sin be the first to throw a stone at her." And once again he bent down and wrote on the ground.

As a scribe or Pharisee, how do you respond inwardly to what Jesus said?

Now identify with Jesus. As you look at the Pharisees and the woman, what do you see as the real issue here? . . . When you bend over, what do you write on the ground?

When they heard it, they went away, one by one, beginning with the elders; and Jesus was left alone with the woman standing before him.

Let yourself become the woman again. What does it feel like to be standing alone before Jesus?

Jesus straightened up and said to her, "Woman, where are they? Has no one condemned you?" She said, "No one, sir." And Jesus said, "Neither do I condemn you. Go your way and from now on do not sin again."

What thoughts and feelings do Jesus' words stir up in you? . . . What do you want to say to Jesus before you go on your way?

Offer five minutes afterward for solitary reflection and invite group members to make notes in their journal about their experience. They will debrief the experience in the Naming portion of the meeting.

➤ Naming: Reflections on Head2Heart (15 minutes)
Debrief with these questions specific to the previous exercise:

- What did you like about the guided imagery? What felt uncomfortable?
- What accusation do you feel hangs over you today?
- Who do you feel needs to be stoned today?
- Whom have you judged, and can you let go of the judgment?

➤ Blessing and Sending Forth (10 minutes)
See page 68 for instructions.

Week 6: Meditating on the Word Together

Preparation for the Meeting

1. See page 63 for additional notes about leader preparation and for the basic outline of this session.

2. *Prepare the materials.* In addition to materials listed on page 64, for the Head2Heart portion of the meeting, you will need: copies of The Group *Lectio* Process handout (page 89) for each participant, travel guide cover materials: magazines to cut up, scissors, butcher paper or paper grocery sacks, tape, glue, markers, crayons, stickers, travel guide dedication prayer on preprinted newsprint for Blessing and Sending Forth. If you intend to continue *The Way of Pilgrimage* next week, have enough copies of Volume 3, *Prayer: Heart of the Pilgrimage*, for all participants.

Note: Both the Naming and Blessing and Sending Forth portions differ from the pattern this week. See page 88.

➤ Welcoming (5 minutes)

See page 64 for instructions.

➤ Noticing: Listening to Your Life (15 minutes)

See page 65 for instructions.

➤ Moving from Head2Heart (10 minutes)

THE HOW-TO

Part 1: GROUP *LECTIO*

Say something like:

Group *lectio* is a process for praying the scripture in small groups. It provides a way to make meditation with scripture the center of a group's meeting time. I have already guided you in personal *lectio* several times in our Head2Heart sessions. Group *lectio* is a variation on what you've already experienced, but it involves you more in the process.

Distribute copies of the Group *Lectio* Process handout printed on page 89, and use it to explain group *lectio divina*. Be sure the group understands when they are to receive shared words without comment and when they are invited to share limited comment. Assure them you will remind them of instructions at each stage.

Guide a group *lectio* experience using Deuteronomy 6:4-9:

• First, assign three persons in addition to yourself to be readers. You, the leader, will be reader #1. Ask the readers to read slowly when you give them the signal, so listeners can hear each word and phrase. Remind listeners before each reading what to pay attention to. Prepare the group members by asking them to become quiet and present to God, waiting in expectancy.

• Remind pilgrims to listen for overall comprehension during the first reading. When you are ready, read the passage.

• After a few moments of silence, ask each person to listen attentively for a particular word or phrase that seems to be given to each. Signal reader #2 to read the passage again. Then after a minute of silence, invite persons to speak aloud the word received. (Remind the group to listen in a spirit of receptivity without comment. When everyone has shared, give guidance about the third reading.)

• Ask the group members to ponder how the passage seems to touch their life. Signal reader #3 to read the same passage again. Then invite each member to speak briefly aloud his or her sense of being touched. (Remind the group to receive these words without comment. When appropriate, give guidance about the fourth reading.)

• Ask the group members to reflect on any invitation they hear in the passage to do or be something in the next few days. Signal reader #4 to read the same passage yet again. Let each person speak of his or her own sense of invitation. Group responses are limited to questions of clarification or brief affirmations, if deeply felt.

• When all have shared, invite the group into a period of prayer. Each person prays aloud for the individual on his or her right—for empowerment to follow through on the invitation. Move around the prayer circle to the left, as each person prays for the person on the right. Group members may pass at any point of sharing in this process. If a person passes on praying aloud, he or she should pray silently and squeeze the hand of the next person when the silent praying is finished.

➤ Naming: Reflections on Head2Heart (15 minutes)

Let group members share their reactions and any new learnings. Say:

We have explored and studied the Bible as a tool and guidebook on our pilgrimage. As a way to close out this unit on the Bible, you will use the supplies provided to create a cover for your Bible, the travel guide. Here are a few questions to help you recall your learnings and insights over the past six weeks:

- **How is the Bible a travel guide for your pilgrimage?**
- **When will you use this travel guide?**
- **Where will this travel guide take you?**

Now participants can proceed to make covers for their Bibles. They can use butcher paper or paper grocery bags to create the covers. They may choose images from magazines or draw on the covers with markers and crayons.

Allow time for everyone to create and to share his or her travel guide cover. Then invite participants to dedicate their covered Bible to their continuing pilgrimage in the Blessing and Sending Forth portion of the meeting.

➤ Blessing and Sending Forth (10 minutes)

Display the following prayer or distribute copies as you stand in a circle. Dedicate the Bibles in one of two ways:

- ask all pilgrims to hold up their Bible to God as you pray; *or*
- place the Bibles in the center of the circle or on the altar before praying

Let us pray:

These Bibles, O God, we dedicate to your purposes. As we offer them to you, so we offer our lives. As you inspired the writers long ago, inspire our reading and hearing of the Word. Strengthen our resolve and encourage our faith that we may be more fully your church in the world. Amen.

THE GROUP *LECTIO* PROCESS

Prepare: Take a moment to become fully present. Sit comfortably alert, close your eyes, and center yourself with breathing.

1. *Hear the word (that is addressed to you).*
First reading (twice). Listen for the word or phrase from the passage that attracts you. Repeat it over to yourself during a one-minute silence. When the leader gives the signal, say aloud only that word or phrase (without elaboration).

2. *Ask, "How is my life touched?"*
Second-stage reading. Listen to discover how this passage touches your life today. Consider possibilities or receive a sensory impression during the two minutes of silence. When the leader gives the signal, speak a sentence or two, perhaps beginning with the words *I hear, I see, I sense.* (Or you may pass.)

3. *Ask, "Is there an invitation here?" (for you).*
Third-stage reading. Listen to discover a possible invitation relevant to the next few days. Ponder it during several minutes of silence. When the leader gives the signal, speak of your sense of invitation. (Or you may pass.)

4. *Pray (for one another's empowerment to respond).*
Pray, aloud or silently, for God to help the person on your right respond to the invitation received.

If desired, group members may share their feelings about the process after completing these steps.

Source: Norvene Vest, *Gathered in the Word: Praying the Scripture in Small Groups* (Nashville, Tenn.: Upper Room Books, 1996), 27. Used by permission for *The Way of Pilgrimage: Leader's Guide.* May be reproduced for group use.

VOLUME 3
PRAYER: HEART OF THE PILGRIMAGE

Repeating Liturgy for Volume 3

You will use this section each week as you work through this volume. It lists all parts that repeat for every session. Review the materials you need to prepare by turning to the first page of each session under "Preparation for the Meeting."

LITURGY OF MEETING

Welcoming
Noticing: Listening to Your Life
Moving from Head2Heart
Naming: Reflections on Head2Heart
Blessing and Sending Forth

Preparation for the Meeting

1. *Prepare yourself spiritually.* Remember you too are a pilgrim on this journey. The best way to prepare for each gathering is to practice living as a pilgrim yourself. Pray specifically for each pilgrim you journey alongside and for God to be present in your time together just as God is present in places of traditional pilgrimage.

2. *Prepare the space.* The space in which you will rest, pray, and share together on your journey is as sacred as places of traditional pilgrimage (such as Notre Dame, the Vatican, or Canterbury). So claim the space as God's sanctuary by placing in it a candle, cross, piece of fabric, icon, or other symbol to remind the group that you gather in the presence of God and to communicate to each pilgrim, "Welcome to this holy place."

3. *Prepare the time.* Being familiar with the readings, exercises, prayers, and practices in the Leader's Guide will help the meeting flow more

smoothly; you will be more more confident in your guiding; and you will have more freedom to let the Spirit move.

4. *Prepare the materials.* Prepare ahead of time small blank pieces of paper rolled up into scrolls (an 8$\frac{1}{2}$ x 11 sheet of paper cut into equal quarters). Cut an equal number of six- to eight-inch pieces of twine or yarn for tying scrolls. These will be used in the Noticing exercise. You will need one scroll for every participant (including yourself), pens, and a basket to hold the scrolls. You will need Bibles and paper. Post closing body prayer and benediction (on page 97) on newsprint or PowerPoint. See each weekly meeting for necessary Head2Heart materials.

—–≈≈≈≈–—

The Welcoming and the Noticing together comprise the opening prayer of the session. Try to allow the first to flow into the next, especially as pilgrims become familiar with the pattern of the meeting and with the exercises themselves. Speaking softly and calmly makes leading exercises easier and can facilitate the flow of the session. Gentle instrumental music in the background may also be beneficial.

Remember that each weekly gathering of the pilgrims is a respite on their journey. Just as towns, churches, and abbeys welcomed pilgrims in earlier times, welcome the group's pilgrims into the meeting and holy space you have created. Before the pilgrims arrive, be attentive to the space: light the candle, have materials set out and prepared, provide water for refreshment; include any elements that communicate: "Welcome! Welcome to this place along the way."

➤ Welcoming (5 minutes)

THE HOW-TO

Offer water and talk quietly to the pilgrims as they arrive. Once everyone has arrived and you are ready to begin, say something like:

Welcome. Welcome to this holy place on your journey. It's good to be here. It's good to have you here. Thank you for coming.

Let's begin first by welcoming Christ into our midst and by praying for the time before us.

Lighting the Candle

Once everyone has been welcomed, allow a little quiet (a holy pause) for people to settle. Invite a pilgrim to light the candle in the room. Say:

> **Leader:**   The Lord be with you.
>
> Other Pilgrims: **And also with you.**

If your group is unfamiliar with this traditional call-and-response, you might introduce it as a way that some more liturgical churches begin prayer. The leader offers a blessing to all present, and the people respond with a blessing for the leader. After the call-and-response, offer the prayer below or one of your choosing.

A PRAYER FOR LIGHT FOR OUR JOURNEY
(Based on Psalm 51 from THE MESSAGE)

God, make a fresh start in us. Create beauty and order from the chaos of our lives. Burn brightly where there is even the tiniest bit of darkness, confusion, and uncertainty. Lord Jesus, shine your light into our hearts as you have already done so on our path. Once again we gather together on this journey to seek you, to find you, to call upon you with all of our heart. Meet us here at this place of rest on our pilgrimage, our Savior and friend. Amen.

➤ Noticing: Listening to Your Life (15 minutes)

One reason for gathering together weekly as pilgrims on the journey is to assist one another in looking back and taking notice. How was God present to us? And what baggage have we been carrying around with us? In this weekly opening exercise, pilgrims will practice looking back through their week. Together they will symbolically leave their "baggage" in a basket (during the time together); then they will name where they noticed God in their week. This exercise encourages being more fully present to God, to one another, and to themselves during the time together.

THE HOW-TO

Guide participants into this segment:

Now we will begin with the Noticing part of our meeting. As we gather together here in this holy space, we want to take a moment to remember where our journeys have taken us this week.

I'd like you to begin by looking back through your week, taking special notice of the moments along the way when you felt most alive. When were you most blessed, joyful, or peaceful? We are often able to recognize God's presence through these kinds of moments.

(Pause for reflection.)

We also want to think about what "baggage" we are still carrying from our week. When I say "baggage," I mean all those things that fill up our minds and weigh down our hearts:

> things we are worried about
> things we have yet to do or yet to finish
> things that left us discouraged
> things that have us bouncing off the walls
> all those things that distract us in one way or another from being truly present in this place emotionally, mentally, and spiritually.

Let's pray. Close your eyes and settle yourself. Take a few deep breaths and let's practice a holy pause together. *(Take a minute or so for this holy pause; you'll know when the pilgrims are settled and ready to engage in the practice of noticing.)* I invite you, in your own way, to ask Jesus to go with you back to the beginning of this week. Recount your journey day by day through the week. If it helps, imagine yourself walking hand in hand with Jesus, looking at the places, the people, the activities, the interactions, the ups and the downs of your journey this week. Answer these questions:

> What brought me joy?
> For what am I grateful?
> What weighed me down this week?
> What drained me?
> What worried me?
> What stressed me out?
> When did I feel hope?

(Allow several minutes for the pilgrims to contemplate these questions.)

Now take one of these scrolls of paper, a pen, and a piece of twine. Unroll the scroll, write down the baggage from your week, then reroll the scroll and tie with the twine. Place your scroll in the basket as an outward sign of inwardly setting aside your baggage in order to enjoy this holy place on your journey and have space to receive what God has to offer you.

(Allow a few minutes for pilgrims to complete this process.)

Let's share briefly one place on our journey this week where we noticed God through blessing, joy, peace, or any other experience. There may be several instances in your week that you could share, but please keep it to one.

Go around the room allowing each pilgrim, including yourself, to share one experience.

—————

Touching Base on Readings/Exercises

What did you notice this past week in the readings and the daily exercises? What do you remember? What stirred you? How did you experience God as you read and practiced the daily exercises?

➤ Moving from Head2Heart (30 minutes)

The intent of this sacred time is to provide space for the message of the daily exercises and readings to move from the mind to the heart—in other words, to move closer to God on this pilgrimage. This segment includes an exercise or practice the group does together. See each weekly gathering for instructions for each Head2Heart exercise.

➤ Naming: Reflections on Head2Heart (15 minutes)

Following the Head2Heart portion comes a time of "naming," in which each pilgrim—alongside companion pilgrims—has the opportunity to articulate and name her or his experience of God through the Head2Heart exercise. Naming is an essential part of the spiritual formation and growth of each pilgrim. Here dots are connected, lightbulbs come on, struggles are affirmed, and journeys intersect.

THE HOW-TO

After completing the Head2Heart exercise, ask the following questions. Have pilgrims answer as they are comfortable. In the first couple of sessions, you might need to explain what naming is and why it's important. Other more specific questions might naturally come from the specific exercise.

- What blessing do you take with you from the exercise we just completed? (That is, what did you learn? What will you take home or carry with you on your journey?)

- How did you experience God during the exercise?
- How/where did you experience the holiness or goodness of God during our gathering today?
- How will these experiences of God encourage you on your continued journey?

➤ Blessing and Sending Forth (10 minutes)

Now it's time for the pilgrims to pack their bags, gather what blessings they have received from this holy space, and move out to continue their journey. Sending them forth to continue their journeys is as important as the welcome. The Blessing and Sending Forth should take five to ten minutes. After the first week, you may adapt the wording to remind pilgrims of the context without repeating the entire introductory paragraph below.

THE HOW-TO

Say:

As we ready ourselves to continue our journey out into the world, we have one more fellow pilgrim to meet. Thérèse was a beautiful young nun who lived in the late 1800s in France. She was also known as "the little flower." She was a teenager when she entered the convent, and she died in her early twenties. She is considered a "doctor" of the Roman Catholic Church for her wisdom, insight, writings, and contributions to the church. One of Thérèse's specialties was prayer. For her, prayer was a surge of the heart— a simple look turned toward heaven, a cry of recognition and of love, embracing both trial and joy. Prayer was something noble, supernatural, that enlarged her soul and united it to God.

Since prayer is the heart of pilgrimage we will close today by practicing prayer as Thérèse teaches us: by lifting the heart and turning it toward God.

Here's how we're going to try this: Let's stand in a circle again. (Wait for everyone to form a circle and become still and quiet.) Everyone take a deep breath, letting all tension fall from our bodies. Now let's close our eyes and breathe again: in and out (speak very slowly) . . . in and out. To breathe is to pray. Let's continue to pray with our breath for just a minute.

(Allow a minute of breathing and praying.)

With our eyes closed, let's imagine for just a moment where God is in the room. And then I want you to imagine lifting and turning your heart toward God. And just keep your heart there before God for just a moment.

(After a minute, close with the following prayer
from the Book of Common Prayer and benediction.)

Heavenly Father, in you we live and move and have our being: We humbly pray you so to guide and govern us by your Holy Spirit, that in all the cares and occupations of our life we may not forget you, but may remember that we are ever walking in your sight; through Jesus Christ our Lord. Amen.[1]

Leader:	Let us go forth into the world continuing on *The Way of Pilgrimage.*
Other Pilgrims:	**Thanks be to God.**

Preparation for the Meeting

1. See page 91 for additional notes about leader preparation and for the basic outline of this session.

2. Prepare the materials: In addition to materials listed on page 92, for the Head2Heart portion of the meeting, you will need: Bibles, journals and extra paper, pens, copies of Finding Your Breath Prayer handout on page 100, drawing paper, crayons and markers, modeling clay or Play-Doh, meditative music CD, CD player, index cards.

Note: The Naming portion of this session features different questions for debriefing the Head2Heart experience. See page 99.

You will notice that the Welcoming prayer and Sending Forth prayer are the same for each week in this volume. Repetition and rhythm are essential parts of the spiritual life. Each week we come as pilgrims from the chaos of life to this centering ritual. Help the pilgrims understand that this repetition is purposeful and necessary. As you repeat various elements week after week, you will find that particular prayers, scriptures, and practices begin to sink from your head to your heart, forming you spiritually in the process.

➤ Welcoming (5 minutes)

See page 92 for instructions.

➤ Noticing: Listening to Your Life (15 minutes)

See page 93 for instructions.

➤ Moving from Head2Heart (30 minutes)

In this session, you will introduce the practice of prayer as the heart of pilgrimage and the secret to life with God. Here pilgrims can "relearn" what prayer is. We have often limited the expanses of prayer by practicing the common approach of beginning with "Dear Lord" and ending with "Amen." In this gathering time we will begin to discover more ways of prayer that open the door into the presence of God.

Begin by asking each pilgrim to respond to the question, *What is prayer to you?* Receive responses for *a few minutes*.

Answers may take the form of what prayer means to participants; what it looks like in their lives; when they pray; or how they experience God in prayer. It's okay if many pilgrims may say that they don't "experience" God in prayer. We are expanding our understanding and practice of prayer together.

Engage the group in exploring prayer in the life of Jesus.

- Quickly form pairs and assign each pair one of the following passages: Luke 2:48-51; Mark 1:35-37; Matthew 11:25-26; Luke 22:41-44; John 11:41-44 or John 17:15-23.
- Ask each pair to consider what the passage says or implies about God's presence to Jesus and how Jesus was present to God in prayer.
- Allow time for the pairs to report back to the full group.

Now invite participants to a period of practicing the presence of God— being attentive and present to the reality of God's presence with us. Say:

We have explored some thoughts on how Jesus was present to God; now we are going to explore our own experience. Take the next fifteen minutes to be quietly present to God in whatever way you feel led (sitting, walking, observing nature, drawing, shaping Play-Doh, journaling, or using a breath prayer [see handout Finding Your Breath Prayer]).

We will gather back in fifteen minutes for some sharing.

Have Play-Doh and art materials available as well as the handout Finding Your Breath Prayer. You could play meditative music in the background, such as music from Taizé.

➤ Naming: Reflections on Head2Heart (15 minutes)

Debrief the Head2Heart experience with these questions:

- How would you describe your experience of being present to God?
- What helps you be present to God?
- What interrupts your presence to God?

➤ Blessing and Sending Forth (10 minutes)

See page 96 for instructions.

FINDING YOUR BREATH PRAYER

A breath prayer is an ancient way of practicing the presence of God, creating an attitude of constant awareness and availability toward God. Here is a way to find your breath prayer:

Spend a few minutes simply paying attention to your breathing. Be still. Let your body release any stress and imagine Jesus standing before you, asking: *What do you want? What do you seek from me?*

Simply respond with the first answer that comes to you. When you've answered, write down your desire.

Next, choose your favorite name for God (Father, Jesus, Lord, Good Shepherd, Abba, Holy One) and write it down.

Now write a one- or two-sentence prayer combining your favorite name for God with your answer to Jesus' question. For example, "Abba Father, let me know your love"; "Good Shepherd, take away my fear"; "Give me peace, O Lord."

Now pray the first half of your prayer as you breathe in and the second half as you breathe out. Continue to practice this prayer for the next few minutes.

You can take this prayer with you into each day, praying it whenever you have a few moments.

Week 2: Discipline of Prayer

Preparation for the Meeting

1. See page 91 for additional notes about leader preparation and for the basic outline of this session.

2. Prepare the materials: In addition to materials listed on page 92, for the Head2Heart portion of the meeting, you will need: Bibles, a large open area to do body prayers, chairs available for Sitting Prayer, a simple worship center with candle and cross, meditative music CD, CD player, your own Bible marked with all ten passages listed for ease of reference; the Lord's Prayer and the Jesus Prayer on newsprint or PowerPoint.

Remember that the Welcoming prayer and Sending Forth prayer are the same for each week of this volume. Help the pilgrims understand that this repetition is purposeful and necessary. As you repeat them week after week, you will find that particular prayers, scriptures, and practices begin to sink from your head to your heart, forming you spiritually in the process.

➤ Welcoming (5 minutes)

See page 92 for instructions.

➤ Noticing: Listening to Your Life (15 minutes)

See page 93 for instructions.

➤ Moving from Head2Heart (30 minutes)

THE HOW-TO

Provide this background:

It has been said that "pilgrims pray with their feet." In fact pilgrims pray with their entire body as they journey from place to place. Part of what has been so powerful and alluring over the centuries is that pilgrimage allows us to offer our prayers, our desires, and our seeking by making a journey with our whole body. Taking our bodies on pilgrimage becomes the outward sign of our inward journeys. So it only makes sense that pilgrims practice using their bodies to express the prayers of their heart.

In the third through fifth centuries, a group of pilgrims known as the desert mothers and fathers fled the cities in the Middle East for the Egyptian and Arabian deserts. They saw society as a "sinking ship" from which they had to swim for their lives. Monasticism (the religious life and communities of monks and nuns) was born here in the desert under direction of a hermit monk named Anthony. The desert mothers and fathers prayed with their entire bodies, through fasting and celibacy, and in other ways as well: Abba Anthony was said to have lifted his arms to the heavens as the sun set and stayed in that prayer posture until the sun rose the next day.

Lead a discussion on praying with our bodies, using these questions:

- Have you ever fasted? Have you ever given up something for Lent? (That's fasting.) Fasting is a classic form of body prayer.
- How or at what other times might you have prayed with your feet or another part of your body?

Read the following scriptures that describe bringing our bodies into prayer and worship. Take note of how the body is used in each scripture:

Exodus 4:31	Psalm 95:6
Exodus 34:8	Psalm 134:2
1 Chronicles 17:16	Daniel 6:10-12
2 Chronicles 6:12-13	Romans 12:1
Nehemiah 9:5-6	1 Timothy 2:8

Exercise

Spread out in the room. If your usual room is small, move to a larger space if possible. A sanctuary also can work well for this exercise. Be sure to have a cross and perhaps a candle in a central place in the room. Meditative music and dimmed lights can lend a nice ambiance. Give the following directions:

We are going to explore praying with our bodies by practicing six different prayer postures. I'll describe the posture and invite you to pray with your body however you'd like. Everyone will hold the posture for a few minutes, then we'll offer the Lord's Prayer together and move on to the next posture. Remember, this is prayer. There isn't any right or wrong way to do this. We're just going to "try out" this way of opening the door into God's presence.

If your group has not memorized the Lord's Prayer, either post it for all to read or substitute a shorter prayer such as the Jesus Prayer: "Jesus Christ, Son of God, have mercy on me, a sinner."

KNEELING PRAYER: **Find a place in the room and kneel. Imagine God before you. Imagine yourself before God. Offer the prayers that rise in your heart as you kneel before God.**

Pause in this posture for a few minutes and then lead the pilgrims in the Lord's Prayer while remaining in the posture.

BOWING DOWN PRAYER: **Find a place in the room and bow down before God. You can stand or kneel. Bowing your head down, honor God. In the quiet, with your head bowed and in your own words, ask God to bless you as a king or queen would bless a bowed knight.**

Pause in this posture for a few minutes and then lead the pilgrims in the Lord's Prayer while remaining in the posture.

UPLIFTED PRAYER: **Find a place in the room and remain standing. Lift up your arms, palms faceup. Close your eyes and lift up your face to God as well. During this time in the quiet, invite the Holy Spirit to fill you as you offer your whole being and your whole life to God. Take a moment to give thanks for God's goodness.**

Pause in this posture for a few minutes and then lead the pilgrims in the Lord's Prayer while remaining in the posture.

SITTING PRAYER: **Find a chair and sit on the ground in front of it. Close your eyes and imagine that you sit at the feet of Jesus. You may want to rest your head on the chair as if resting your head on his lap. This time in the quiet, listen for what Jesus might be saying to you as you rest.**

Pause in this posture for a few minutes and then lead the pilgrims in the Lord's Prayer while remaining in the posture.

SOAKING PRAYER: **Find a place on the floor and lie down flat on your back. Place your arms at your side with palms faceup once again. Close your eyes and notice your breathing. In this quiet, imagine with every breath that you sink deeper and deeper into the presence of God (as if soaking in a bathtub or falling backward into a swimming pool). From your head to your feet, invite the Holy Spirit to bring peace to your body.**

Pause in this posture for a few minutes and then lead the pilgrims in the Lord's Prayer while remaining in the posture.

SURRENDER PRAYER: **Finally, turn onto your stomach, extending your arms out above your head. Keep your head facedown. In the quiet, surrender** yourself to God. Name before God those parts in your life that need "to be laid down." Remember how Christ laid down his life (his body) for you.

Pause in this posture for a few minutes and then lead the pilgrims in the Lord's Prayer while remaining in the posture.

➤ Naming: Reflections on Head2Heart (15 minutes)

Have the pilgrims reassemble. Ask which postures most helped them feel God's presence. What was it like to pray with their body? See page 95 for instructions.

➤ Blessing and Sending Forth (10 minutes)

See page 96 for instructions.

Preparation for the Meeting

1. See page 91 for additional notes about leader preparation and for the basic outline of this session.

2. Prepare the materials: In addition to materials listed on page 92, for the Head2Heart portion of the meeting, you will need: journals and extra paper. For optional exercise: set up circle of chairs in groups of four or five with one extra chair in the middle.

Remember to help the pilgrims understand that repetition of the Welcoming and Sending Forth prayers is purposeful. As you repeat them week after week, you will find that particular prayers, scriptures, and practices begin to sink from your head to your heart, forming you spiritually in the process.

➤ Welcoming (5 minutes)

See page 92 for instructions.

➤ Noticing: Listening to Your Life (15 minutes)

See page 93 for instructions.

➤ Moving from Head2Heart (30 minutes)

Set a context for a guided experience of intercessory prayer based on Mark 2:1-12.

THE HOW-TO

- Read Mark 2:1-12 aloud for the group. Invite the group to focus on verses 1-5.
- Ask the group what this story might teach us about praying on behalf of others.

Some insights you might draw out include the following:

a) Sometimes we have no faith for ourselves; we need others to have faith for us. In healing the paralytic, Jesus honors the faith and love of the four for their friend.

b) The role of the four was not to cure their friend but to care for him and to carry him into the healing presence of Jesus. That is our role also in intercessory prayer.

c) The care of the four was evident in their active willingness to go out of their way and to persevere in love for their friend. Love (not our diagnosis or instructions to God) is the content of prayer for others. We unite our spirits with Christ to be vessels through whom God loves the world.

d) There are factors in and among us (the crowd, the cynics, the roofing) that keep people from God, that obstruct love and intercession, so prayer requires a love that perseveres.

Lead the group in intercessory prayer guided by images from this story.

- Ask everyone to find a comfortable place to sit or lie down where he or she can enter into an attitude of prayer.
- Acknowledge that God is with us and invites us to offer ourselves as vessels of divine presence to others.
- Assure the pilgrims that it is all right to follow their own way of reflecting if they have difficulty visualizing what is being suggested.
- After another moment of silence, guide their prayer slowly and gently with directions like these:

Imagine yourself as one of the four persons holding a corner of a stretcher. Take note of whom God places on the stretcher for you to help carry. Whom is God calling you to care for, to help carry into God's presence today? Just take a moment to see the person and receive him or her in love.

(Pause thirty seconds.)

Imagine yourself carrying your friend toward Jesus. And notice any ways the path for your friend seems obstructed. How are you frustrated in your effort to care for this person? Who or what gets in the way?

(Pause thirty seconds.)

And now imagine yourself persevering in your intent to care for your friend and to bring her or him into Jesus' presence. Dig through the roofing that separates your friend and you from Jesus and the healing your friend needs. Take notice: are there many layers? If so, what are they?

(Pause thirty seconds.)

Lower your friend into Jesus' presence. Watch and see how Jesus receives

your friend, what he does and what he says. And see your friend being restored to wholeness in the radiance of divine love.

(Pause one minute.)

And now release your friend to God's care. Give thanks to God. And return to your home.

(Pause one minute and say "Amen.")

Give the group members a few more minutes in silence to reflect on their prayer and to write in their journals. Then ask the pilgrims to turn to another person to share something they received or something that caused them to struggle.

OPTIONAL: Invite the group to enter into a second experience of prayer: silent healing prayer for one another.

- Say words like: **We are accustomed to praying for one another with many words, but words can hinder as well as help the flow of God's love. Perhaps you would like to be on that stretcher, carried by friends to Jesus. You will have that opportunity now, if you choose.**
- Form groups of four or five. Guide them as simply as possible.
- Sit or stand in circles with an empty chair in the center of each circle.
- As a person wishes to be "on the stretcher" to be carried into Jesus' restorative presence, he or she sits in the center chair. The person may express a need aloud if desired, but there is no need to do so. Emphasize also that it is okay to participate without choosing to sit in the center chair for prayer.
- Fellow pilgrims stand and silently place their hands on the person's head and shoulders and carry the person into Jesus' presence in the prayer of their hearts. No prayers are spoken.
- After a few minutes, the person in the center signals readiness to stand, and all return to the circle. This pattern continues until everyone who chooses to has had a chance to present himself or herself for prayer.

➤ Naming: Reflections on Head2Heart (15 minutes)

See page 95 for instructions.

➤ Blessing and Sending Forth (10 minutes)

See page 96 for instructions.

Week 4: Praying the Psalms

Preparation for the Meeting

1. See page 91 for additional notes about leader preparation and for the basic outline of this session.
2. Prepare the materials: In addition to materials listed on page 92, for the Head2Heart portion of the meeting, you will need: Bibles, paper, pencils and pens.

➤ Welcoming (5 minutes)

See page 92 for instructions.

➤ Noticing: Listening to Your Life (15 minutes)

See page 93 for instructions.

➤ Moving from Head2Heart (30 minutes)

Say words like: **Psalms express corporate prayer as well as personal prayer. They help us to pray in communion with God's people in every age who have prayed the same psalms. The Psalms allow an honest expression of ourselves in prayer to God. We are going to prepare for prayer with Psalm 23 by reflecting on what it means in a rather unusual way—through a reverse paraphrase.**

THE HOW-TO

- Invite each pilgrim to write a reverse paraphrase of Psalm 23. Explain that a reverse paraphrase is writing lines that represent the opposite of what each verse or stanza means to you. For example, a person might reverse "The Lord is my shepherd" to say, "I have no God to guide me" or "There is no God." The value lies in helping us discover the real power of familiar words in a fresh way. Remind everyone that this is not a literary contest. There is no right or wrong way of doing it, only personal expression.
- Share reverse paraphrases. Ask everyone to return to the circle and, if willing, to share his or her reverse paraphrase of Psalm 23. Following

each paraphrase, you might say together, "The Lord is my shepherd, I shall not want." Be prepared for the despair that can be communicated through a reverse paraphrase of this psalm. Ask participants if they know or can imagine people who feel this way and experience life "having no hope and without God in the world" (Eph. 2:12).

- Now invite the group to hear the grace in Psalm 23 afresh and to let the words of the psalm guide the group in a period of prayer. Explain that we will let the psalm guide our prayer time, one verse at a time. Following each verse, anyone may express prayers to God with positive paraphrases of the verse, petitions and intercessions, or other personal responses that the verse evokes. For example, Psalm 23:1 might inspire "O God, you are my shepherd and guide," "Lord, you have shepherded me even without my knowing it; I have ignored you most of my life," or "Shepherd of souls, find and guide my sister." Or the Spirit may move someone to sing a song to God. Begin with a moment of silent prayer, then read Psalm 23 verse by verse. Allow sufficient time for pilgrims to soak in the meaning of the verse and offer their responses.

- Conclude the time of prayer by having everyone read Psalm 23 in unison.

➤ Naming: Reflections on Head2Heart (15 minutes)
See page 95 for instructions.

➤ Blessing and Sending Forth (10 minutes)
See page 96 for instructions.

Week 5: Prayer Practices from Our Tradition

Preparation for the Meeting

1. See page 91 for additional notes about leader preparation and for the basic outline of this session.
2. Prepare the materials: In addition to materials listed on page 92, for the Head2Heart portion of the meeting, you will need: drawings, photographs, or paintings (from the Internet, magazines, art books, etc.) of real people and situations that convey human feeling and a variety of human conditions, Head2Heart questions on page 111 printed on newsprint or copied for each participant, journals and extra paper, pens.

Note: The Naming portion of this session uses a different format in order to debrief the specific exercise in Head2Heart. See page 112.

➤ Welcoming (5 minutes)
See page 92 for instructions.

➤ Noticing: Listening to Your Life (15 minutes)
See page 93 for instructions.

➤ Moving from Head2Heart (30 minutes)

In our own way we all journey through this life with the hopeful expectation that we will find writing on the wall, flashing neon signs dropped from the sky, or a booming voice when we need to hear from God. But we know that although God is capable of such means of communication, more often than not God speaks to us in the still small voice within.

In 1 Kings 19 Elijah experiences the wind, the earthquake, and then the fire, none of which contained God. But when Elijah heard that still small voice he knew the company of God (KJV). As pilgrims, we seek to pay attention to God's voice and presence, no matter what the form. But hearing that still small voice whispering within and around us is hard when our lives are very loud and very full. So we need to practice the art of being quiet, of being still and stepping back from our full, loud lives in order to hear the voice of God echoing to us.

Introduce today's practice as one that helps us tune into God's voice and presence by being quiet, being still, and stepping away from our crazy lives. Traditionally this prayer has been called the practice of silence and solitude. Begin by reading the story of Elijah in 1 Kings 19:9-12 (KJV).

- Ask if anyone has heard God speak through a "still small voice"
- Begin to imagine together what God's "still small voice" might look like in our lives. What do we need to do be able to hear God's "still small voice"?

Exercise

Lead the group in an exercise of active prayer: seeing and responding to God in human life.

- Place facedown on a table a number of drawings, photographs, or paintings (from magazines, art books, for example) of real people and situations that convey human feeling and a variety of human conditions.
- Invite pilgrims to select a picture at random and accept it as their focus for prayerful reflection and listening to God.
- Ask the pilgrims to spend time gazing at their pictures and then to reflect in their journals on the following questions:
  1. What do I see, hear, and feel? What is the human story behind the picture? (*Encounter life.*)
  2. What passage of scripture comes to mind, and what is the connection? (*Reflect on life in light of the Word.*)
  3. What does Christ see, hear, feel, and want to do? Write a conversation with Christ about one of the pictures and what it represents for you both. (*Discern the presence of Christ.*)
  4. What is Christ saying to you (and to us) through this experience? (*Respond to God's call.*)

Gather the group together for sharing.

- Invite all to share their responses to this exercise: pictures and the feelings/stories they evoked, scriptures, and conversations with Christ.
- After all have shared, ask participants to be quiet where they are for three minutes, simply listening for God's call:

How is God speaking to you through this experience—questioning, blessing, challenging you? Write your impressions in your journal.

➤ Naming: Reflections on Head2Heart (15 minutes)

Bring the group back together to process the experience. Ask:

1. How does being still help you see or hear God in the world?
2. How can you develop a discipline of silence and solitude in your life?
3. How can you practice seeing the world through God's eyes as you have done in this exercise?

Close the time by reading Psalm 131 together.

➤ Blessing and Sending Forth (10 minutes)

See page 96 for instructions.

Week 6: Practicing Creative Prayer

Preparation for the Meeting

1. See page 91 for additional notes about leader preparation and for the basic outline of this session.
2. Prepare the materials: In addition to materials listed on page 92, for the Head2Heart portion of the meeting, you will need to set up the room with prayer stations before the session begins. *Crayons*: table, chairs, paper, crayons; *Pens*: table, chairs, paper (or stationery), envelopes, journals, pens; *Pillows*: beanbag chairs or large pillows to sit on; *Cross*: have a large cross in an open area, fabric under cross, candle (optional). *Music*: CD players and headphones, meditative CDs or contemporary Christian music.

➤ Welcoming (5 minutes)
See page 92 for instructions.

➤ Noticing: Listening to Your Life (15 minutes)
See page 93 for instructions.

➤ Moving from Head2Heart (30 minutes)
For the past five weeks your group has been practicing various ways of prayer. You have prayed with your bodies; with crayons; by walking and by being still; by writing and by listening. In this last gathering, pilgrims will practice the prayer of their choice based on how the Spirit moves them. You will need to set up the prayer stations ahead of time for this gathering. Meditative music played softly will also help keep pilgrims in the place of prayer.

THE HOW-TO

Begin with a quick wrap-up discussion based on the following questions:

- **Which prayer exercise have you liked the best?** (You may want to review them.)
- **How has your view of prayer changed over the last five weeks?**

- How has this broader view of prayer affected your prayer life and daily life?
- Why do you think prayer is the heart of pilgrimage? What makes it essential?

Exercise

Begin by telling the pilgrims that they'll get to choose today how they pray, using the various methods they have practiced through the week. Explain the five prayer stations set up in the room:

1. CRAYONS: **where you can draw and/or color on the paper provided;**
2. PENS: **where you can journal or write letters on the paper provided;**
3. PILLOWS: **where you can sit and be still before God;**
4. CROSS: **where you can use prayer postures to express your prayer;**
5. MUSIC: **where you can hear prayer and praise through instruments and voice.**

Continue with directions like these:

This is your time to pray, so pray however you feel moved. I will read a few verses at a time from the Gospel of Matthew and then pause. In the pause, you will choose one station and pray as you feel led by the scripture verses. Please wait and listen a moment before deciding where and how to pray. After five to six minutes, I will read another verse, and you can select another station. It's OK for several of you to be at one station, but try to balance out numbers at each. You can also stay at just one or two stations if you prefer.

Begin with a minute or two of quiet before God—to turn your hearts toward God. Then read:

• Matthew 6:5-6	Pause; allow four minutes
• Matthew 6:7-8	Pause; allow four minutes
• Matthew 6:9-13	Pause; allow four minutes
• Matthew 6:19-21	Pause; allow four minutes
• Matthew 6:31-33	Pause; allow four minutes

Conclude by calling pilgrims back together and rereading the entire passage (Matthew 6:5-13, 19-21, 31-33), concluding with "**the Word of God. Amen.**"

➤ Naming: Reflections on Head2Heart (15 minutes)

Allow pilgrims to share their experience in prayer with one another. How did they experience God's presence? What were they drawn to? How did God speak to them?

➤ Blessing and Sending Forth (10 minutes)

See page 96 for instructions.

VOLUME 4
COMPANIONS ON THE PILGRIMAGE

Repeating Liturgy for Volume 4

You will use this section each week as you work through this volume. It lists all parts that repeat for every session. Review the materials you need to prepare by turning to the first page of each session under "Preparation for the Meeting."

LITURGY OF MEETING

Welcoming
Noticing: Listening to Your Life
Moving from Head2Heart
Naming: Reflections on Head2Heart
Blessing and Sending Forth

Preparation for the Meeting

1. *Prepare yourself spiritually.* Remember you too are a pilgrim on this journey. The best way to prepare for each gathering is to practice living as a pilgrim yourself. Pray specifically for each pilgrim you journey alongside and for God to be present in your time together just as God is present in places of traditional pilgrimage.

2. *Prepare the space.* The space in which you will rest, pray, and share together on your journey is as sacred as places of traditional pilgrimage (such as Notre Dame, the Vatican, or Canterbury). So claim the space as God's sanctuary by placing in it a candle, cross, piece of fabric, icon, or other symbol to remind the group that you gather in the presence of God and to communicate to each pilgrim, "Welcome to this holy place."

3. *Prepare the time.* Being familiar with the readings, exercises, prayers, and practices in the Leader's Guide will help the meeting flow more smoothly; you will be more more confident in your guiding; and you will have more freedom to let the Spirit move.

4. *Prepare the materials.* Prepare ahead of time small blank pieces of paper rolled up into scrolls (an 8½ x 11 sheet of paper cut into equal quarters is a good size). Cut an equal number of six- to eight-inch pieces of twine or yarn for tying scrolls. These will be used in the Noticing exercise. You will need one scroll for every participant (including yourself), pens, and a basket to hold the scrolls. You will need Bibles and paper. Post closing prayer and benediction on newsprint or PowerPoint. See each weekly meeting for necessary Head2Heart materials.

***

The Welcoming and the Noticing together comprise the opening prayer of the session. Try to allow the first to flow into the next. Speaking softly and calmly makes leading exercises easier and can facilitate the flow of the session. Gentle instrumental music in the background may also be beneficial.

Remember that each weekly gathering of the pilgrims is a respite on their journey. Just as towns, churches, and abbeys welcomed pilgrims in earlier times, welcome the group's pilgrims into the meeting and holy space you have created. Before the pilgrims arrive, be attentive to the space: light the candle, have materials set out and prepared, provide water for refreshment; include any elements that communicate: "Welcome! Welcome to this place along the way."

➤ Welcoming (5 minutes)

THE HOW-TO

Offer water and talk quietly to the pilgrims as they arrive. Once everyone has arrived and you are ready to begin, say something like:

Welcome. Welcome to this holy place on your journey. It's good to be here. It's good to have you here. Thank you for coming.

Let's begin first by welcoming Christ into our midst and by praying for the time before us.

Lighting the Candle
Once everyone has been welcomed, allow a little quiet (a holy pause) for people to settle. Invite a pilgrim to light the candle in the room. Say:

Leader:	The Lord be with you.
Other Pilgrims:	**And also with you.**

If your group is unfamiliar with this traditional call-and-response, you might introduce it as a way that some more liturgical churches begin prayer. The leader offers a blessing to all present, and the people respond with a blessing for the leader. After the call-and-response, offer the prayer below or one of your choosing.

A PRAYER FOR LIGHT FOR OUR JOURNEY

Almighty God, you have surrounded us with a great cloud of witnesses who still emit such great light for our paths. Grant that in our earthly pilgrimage we may always be supported by this fellowship of love and prayer as we persevere in running the race that you have placed before each of us. Amen.[1]

➤ Noticing: Listening to Your Life (15 minutes)

One reason for gathering together weekly as pilgrims on the journey is to assist one another in looking back and taking notice. How was God present to people? And what baggage have pilgrims been carrying around? In this weekly opening exercise, pilgrims will practice looking back through the week. Together they will symbolically leave their "baggage" in a basket (during the time together); then they will name where they noticed God in their week. This exercise encourages being more fully present to God, to one another, and to themselves during the group meeting time.

THE HOW-TO

Guide participants into this segment:

Now we will begin the Noticing part of our meeting. As we gather together here in this holy space, we want to take a moment to remember where our journeys have taken us this week.

I'd like you to begin by looking back through your week, taking special notice of the moments along the way when you felt most alive. When were you most blessed, joyful, or peaceful? We are often able to recognize God's presence through these kinds of moments.

(Pause for reflection.)

We also want to think about what "baggage" we are still carrying from our week. When I say "baggage," I mean all those things that fill up our minds and weigh down our hearts:

> things we are worried about
> things we have yet to do or yet to finish

things that left us discouraged
things that have us bouncing off the walls
all those things that distract us in one way or another from being truly
present in this place emotionally, mentally, and spiritually present.

Let's pray. Close your eyes and settle yourself. Take a few deep breaths and let's practice a holy pause together. *(Take a minute or so for this holy pause; you'll know when the pilgrims are settled and ready to engage in the practice of noticing.)* I invite you, in your own way, to ask Jesus to go with you back to the beginning of this week. Recount your journey day by day through the week. If it helps, imagine yourself walking hand in hand with Jesus, looking at the places, the people, the activities, the interactions, the ups and the downs of your journey this week. Answer these questions:

What brought me joy?
For what am I grateful?
What weighed me down this week?
What drained me?
What worried me?
What stressed me out?
When did I feel hope?

(Allow several minutes for the pilgrims to contemplate these questions.)

Now take one of these scrolls of paper, a pen, and a piece of twine. Unroll the scroll, write down the baggage from your week, then reroll the scroll and tie with the twine. Place your scroll in the basket as an outward sign of inwardly setting aside your baggage in order to enjoy this holy place on your journey and have space to receive what God has to offer you.

(Allow a few minutes for pilgrims to complete this process.)

Let's share briefly with one place on our journey this week where we noticed God through blessing, joy, peace, or any other experience. There may be several instances in your week that you could share, but please keep it to one.

Go around the room allowing each pilgrim, including yourself, to share one experience.

<hr />

Touching Base on Readings/Exercises

What did you notice this past week in the readings and the daily exercises? What do you remember? What stirred you? How did you experience God as you read and practiced the daily exercises?

➤ Moving from Head2Heart (30 minutes)

The intent of this sacred time is to provide space for the message of the daily exercises and readings to move from the mind to the heart—in other words, to move closer to God on this pilgrimage. This segment includes an exercise or practice the group does together. See each weekly gathering for instructions for each Head2Heart exercise.

➤ Naming: Reflections on Head2Heart (15 minutes)

Following the Head2Heart portion comes a time of "naming," in which each pilgrim—alongside companion pilgrims—has the opportunity to articulate and name her or his experience of God through the Head2Heart exercise. Naming is an essential part of the spiritual formation and growth of each pilgrim. Here dots are connected, lightbulbs come on, struggles are affirmed, and journeys intersect.

THE HOW-TO

After completing the Head2Heart exercise, ask the following questions. Have pilgrims answer as they are comfortable. In the first couple of sessions, you might need to explain what naming is and why it's important. Other more specific questions might naturally come from the specific exercise.

- **What blessing do you take with you from the exercise we just completed? (That is, what did you learn? What will you take home or carry with you on your journey?)**
- How did you experience God during the exercise? Or, how did you experience God's presence?
- How/where did you experience the holiness or goodness of God during our gathering today?
- How will these experiences of God encourage you on your continued journey?

➤ Blessing and Sending Forth (10 minutes)

Now it's time for the pilgrims to pack their bags, gather what blessings they have received from this holy space, and move out to continue their journey. Sending them forth to continue their journeys is as important as the welcome. The Blessing and Sending Forth should take five to ten minutes.

Have available index cards and pencils for those who want to use them as a reminder of their prayer partner, and copies of the closing prayer and benediction for each person (if not posted for all to see).

Have everyone stand in a circle. Say words like these:

One way we stay together on pilgrimage as we leave this place and continue on our own journeys is through prayer. Dr. Christina Verneuil, who practices medicine in rural Alaska, says, "Prayer is what keeps us together no matter how far apart we live or travel."[2] And so we are going to pay attention to our traveling companions this week through prayer as a way of continuing to walk together while we are apart. The person on your right will be the pilgrim for whom you pray daily this week. Go ahead and write down the name of the person if you'd like. Remember that prayer keeps us together on this journey. So don't forget to pray for your traveling companion this week.

Now let's practice praying for each other while we're all still together. As we remain in the circle, I'd like you to place your right hand lightly on the upper back of your traveling companion for the week (the person on your right).

Closing Prayer

Let us pray together:

Into your hands, O Lord God, we commend our friends. Thank you for the gift of their companionship on this pilgrimage. We lift to you their hearts, their minds, and their bodies. We ask you to meet them in their worries and struggles; in their work and in their rest; in their joy and in their peace. Remind us that we not only walk with you on this journey but we also walk with one another. Amen.

Benediction

Leader:	Let us go forth into the world continuing on *The Way of Pilgrimage.*
Other Pilgrims:	**Thanks be to God.**

Week 1: Those Who Have Traveled Before Us

Preparation for the Meeting

1. See page 117 for additional notes about leader preparation.
2. Prepare the materials: In addition to materials listed on page 118, for the Head2Heart portion of the meeting, you will need: space to set up six prayer stations; copies of the pictures and biographies of saints listed on pages 126–28 (copy descriptions and find images at www.upper room.org/methodx/thelife/saints.asp or search on Google Images); journals; copies of the three questions on page 125 at each of the six stations; paragraph on saints from *The Upper Room Dictionary of Christian Spiritual Formation* (printed on page 124) copied for each person or on PowerPoint.If you decide to do the extra activity, you need a TV, DVD player, and the movie *Thérèse: The Story of Saint Thérèse of Lisieux* (www.theresemovie.com).

You will notice that the Welcoming prayer and Sending Forth prayer are the same for each week in this volume. Repetition and rhythm are essential parts of the spiritual life. Each week we come as pilgrims from the chaos of life to this centering ritual. Help the pilgrims understand that this repetition is purposeful and necessary. As you repeat various elements week after week, you will find that particular prayers, scriptures, and practices begin to sink from your head to your heart, forming you spiritually in the process.

➤ Welcoming (5 minutes)
See page 118 for instructions.

➤ Noticing: Listening to Your Life (15 minutes)
See page 119 for instructions.

THE HOW-TO

Say something like:

Although each of us travels on our own pilgrimage, thankfully we don't walk alone. Pilgrimage allows us to keep company with a wider group of traveling companions beyond those we see with our eyes. Pilgrimage involves walking in the footsteps of all the faithful who have come before us, the pioneers of faith have blazed the spiritual path home for us. In the church we call this band of pilgrims "the great cloud of witnesses." So on pilgrimage, the great saints and the ordinary saints become our guides along the way.

Jesus wasn't kidding when he said that those who believe in him have everlasting life. Through him we live with all the faithful who have gone before us. It can boggle our minds to think how our lives are much bigger than the moments we live in, and our relationships go beyond the people whose hands we can physically hold on to. We are part of the communion of saints across all boundaries of time and space. In fact, our very own cheering squad, our personal prayer team, surrounds us. A stadium full of God's saints is rooting us on, nudging us forward, calling each of us by name as they encourage us to hang in there, to stay in the race, not to lose hope.

Exercise

The Celtic church believed that the space between heaven and earth—between this world and the next—was very thin. So they befriended saints who were no longer on this earth and walked through life with them, just as we walk through this life with family and friends.

Begin by reading together the explanation of saints below from *The Upper Room Dictionary of Christian Spiritual Formation*. Help your group understand that saints like Teresa of Ávila and Thérèse of Lisieux were not perfect human beings but examples of lives lived faithfully in every moment—examples worthy of examining and emulating.

Saints were and are ordinary people. Though imperfect, doubt-filled, weak, lonely, and fearful at times, they chose to remain uncompromisingly faithful witnesses to the gospel. This great "cloud of witnesses" (Hebrews 12:1) is the unity of all believers past, present, and future. There are no boundaries or barriers to inclusiveness, not even between living and dead. . . . These ordinary folks make loving God and neighbor their extraordinary choice day in and day out. . . . Saints step out in faith, trusting and obeying the call of God."[3]

Now direct the group to the six stations around the room dedicated to the saints described on pages 126–28. Be sure to include a picture and brief biography of each saint. Ask the group to spread out around the room, read about the lives of two or three saints they feel drawn to, and contemplate their pictures. Invite them to consider the following questions as they travel briefly with several of these saints. They should take their journal to each station and write their reflections and thoughts:

- Do you see any similarities between your life and this saint's life?
- What is radically different from your life?
- What aspect of this person's life inspires you to live your own life more faithfully?

Once pilgrims have spent time with the saints, draw the group together to share reflections. Ask which saint each pilgrim wants to accompany him or her in the coming week. Have extra pictures of the saints and let the pilgrims take a picture home as a reminder of what they learned and how they are challenged.

THE SAINTS

Mother Teresa of Calcutta

Born in 1910, Mother Teresa knew early on that she was called to help the poor. She became a nun and taught at a girls' college in Calcutta until 1946, when she left her convent to help the poorest of the poor while living among them. In her Home for Dying Destitutes, she provided a shelter where the poor could die in dignity. As founder and leader of the Missionaries of Charity, Mother Teresa's attitude toward money was that God would provide whatever she needed. "Money, I never think of it," she once said. "It always comes. The Lord sends it. We do his work; he provides the means. If he does not give us the means, that shows he does not want the work. So why worry?" A favorite motto she lived and preached was "Do small things with great love." She was awarded the Nobel Peace Prize in 1979.

Francis of Assisi

Most people think of Francis of Assisi, born sometime around 1181, as a sweet, simple man who picked flowers and talked with animals. He was much more than that. As a young man he willingly went to war and eventually was imprisoned. Once while on the way to a battle, Francis heard a divine voice inviting him to start serving the master rather than the servant. It was then he decided to live for God alone.

Decision by decision Francis stripped himself of attachments, to be more like Jesus. In his early twenties, Francis decided to become like the poor he met in Assisi's backstreets. One day, while praying, he heard a voice say, "Go and repair my church." Thinking that he was to fix the dilapidated church of Saint Damian, he set to work. This infuriated his father, who took him to the bishop's court, demanding that his son repay the money he had spent on repairs. Francis then stripped naked, returning his clothes to his father as a sign that he was letting go of his family and his inheritance. He spent the rest of his life until his death in 1226 preaching and healing, attracting followers by his unflagging devotion to Christ.

Catherine of Siena

Saint Catherine of Siena was born in 1347 to a family that already had twenty-three children. Early on, she identified herself as an activist, even cutting off her hair to show her parents that she vehemently refused to marry. She developed a habit of self-imposed solitude, only emerging for mass. At age eighteen she joined a group of women called the Mantellate, who served the poor and sick in the community. Two years later she had a mystical experience that caused her to devote her life solely to God.

Catherine became widely sought after for her theological viewpoints and ability to interpret the Bible, and even the Pope asked for her counsel. Her thoughts survive in her work *Dialogue*, in which she sets up a theological debate with God. In it she develops love and truth as the only ways to strive for the perfection of God. Catherine always labored first out of love for God. After years of fasting and penance, she died when she was only thirty-three.

Teresa of Ávila

Saint Teresa spent much of her early life in consternation because she considered herself to be too great a sinner. She was sent to a monastery when she was sixteen years old, and while put off by this lifestyle at first, she ultimately chose a nun's life over marriage because she thought it was the only way to keep herself from sinning. When Teresa became disillusioned with her convent at age forty-three, she moved out to start her own, a place where quiet reflection and mental prayer were stressed.

Teresa was always more keen on working than on theorizing. She let her love of God shine through her deeds more than her words. For twenty years before her death in 1582, she was instrumental in establishing seventeen Carmelite convents in Spain and helped to revitalize Christianity in her area. Her first major work, *The Way of Perfection*, provided sisters in her convents with practical guidelines on how to pray and live together in Christian community. Her most famous book, *The Interior Castle*, describes seven stages of prayer as we grow toward union with God. Teresa is remembered as a reformer, mystic, and person of great character and humor.

Martin Luther

Martin Luther (1483–1546) was a German monk, priest, professor, theologian, and church reformer. His teachings inspired the Reformation and deeply influenced the doctrines and culture of the Lutheran and other Protestant traditions, as well as the course of Western civilization.

Martin Luther dealt the symbolic blow that began the Reformation when he nailed his Ninety-Five Theses to the door of the Wittenberg Church. That document contained an attack on papal abuses and the sale of indulgences by church officials.

But Luther himself saw the Reformation as something far more important than a revolt against ecclesiastical abuses. He believed it was a fight for the gospel. Luther even stated that he would have happily yielded every point of dispute to the pope, if only the pope had affirmed the gospel.

And at the heart of the gospel, in Luther's estimation, was the doctrine of justification by faith—the teaching that Christ's own righteousness is imputed to those who believe, and on that ground alone, they are accepted by God.

Martin Luther King Jr.

Until the 1960s African Americans living in many parts of the United States did not have the same rights and privileges as other citizens. Most were denied access to the same education, health care, and decent homes as other people. In 1964 Congress passed the Civil Rights Act, making it illegal to separate people because of race, but many people still mistreated African Americans and would not accept them as equals.

Dr. Martin Luther King Jr., a Baptist minister in Georgia and Alabama, talked about his dream that one day all children would be treated the same, since they are all members of God's family. He organized nonviolent demonstrations and led people to march, sing, and pray for change. Dr. King continued to lead people although he was beaten and thrown into jail. Finally he was assassinated in 1968. Dr. King had led his followers to practice the active love of Jesus. American people and society changed because of his leadership.

Suggested Resources on Saints

Servants, Misfits, and Martyrs: Saints and Their Stories by James C. Howell (Nashville, Tenn.: Upper Room Books, 1999)

The Upper Room Spiritual Classics Series (Nashville, Tenn.: Upper Room Books)

Under Her Wings: Spiritual Guidance from Women Saints by Kathy Bence (Nashville, Tenn.: Upper Room Books, 2001)

Lesser Feasts and Fasts (New York: Church Publishing, Inc., annual)

Brightest and Best: A Companion to the Lesser Feasts and Fasts by Sam Portaro (Cambridge, Mass.: Cowley Publications, 1997)

➤ Naming: Reflections on Head2Heart (15 minutes)

See page 121 for instructions.

➤ Blessing and Sending Forth (10 minutes)

See page 121 for instructions.

➤ A Highly Recommended Extra for This Session

If you can plan a longer time frame for this session or can schedule a movie night, we recommend watching all or part of the movie *Thérèse: The Story of Saint Thérèse of Lisieux* (http://www.theresemovie.com/). The film runs 94 minutes. This movie will give pilgrims a clearer picture of a saint who was also a young person drawn to God.

After you watch the movie, debrief with these questions, allowing one to two minutes for response to each:

- Do you see any similarities between your life story and Thérèse's?
- What is radically different from your life?
- What aspect of her life could inspire you to live your own life more faithfully?

Week 2: Those Who Travel with Us

Preparation for the Meeting

1. See page 117 for additional notes about leader preparation.
2. Prepare the materials: In addition to materials listed on page 118, for the Head2Heart portion of the meeting, you will need: index cards, pens, a bell, copies of the Holy Listening handout (pages 133–34), and a tea light or votive candle (and candleholder) for each person.

Note: The Naming portion differs from the usual. See page 131.

Remember that the Welcoming prayer and Sending Forth prayer are the same for each week of this volume. Help the pilgrims understand that this repetition is purposeful and necessary. As you repeat them week after week, you will find that particular prayers, scriptures, and practices begin to sink from your head to your heart, forming you spiritually in the process.

➤ Welcoming (5 minutes)

See page 118 for instructions.

➤ Noticing: Listening to Your Life (15 minutes)

See page 119 for instructions.

➤ Moving from Head2 Heart (30 minutes)

Say something like:

Look around the room for a moment. Look at the pilgrims who gather here each week and are making this journey with you. These are the most easily recognized of your traveling companions.

There is a difference between a group of friends and a band of pilgrims. Friends tend to focus inward on one another or on a common activity. Pilgrims stand side by side and look outward together. They focus not on one another but on God whom they each seek, and on the journey before them. Of course, bands of pilgrims laugh, talk, share, cry, and do many of the things a group of friends does. But they do more. They know a deeper connection exists among pilgrims because of the spiritual journey they make together.

Exercise

Pair the pilgrims and give each pair about thirty minutes to practice being a spiritual friend and traveling companion. Have each pair share briefly and write on a note card several significant things in each other's upcoming week—the joys and struggles of each person—and what each needs on this pilgrimage of faith.

Distribute copies of the Holy Listening Reflection Sheet. Say something like:

Listening deeply to another person places us on sacred ground. The person we listen to is a child of God, made in the divine image. Moreover, God is present with us when we listen deeply to one of God's precious children. So we can also listen for God as we listen to the other person. We can pay attention to how God is present for and through the other and how God is present to us personally in the time of listening.

Introduce the holy listening exercise, explaining the basic steps of holy listening as outlined on the handout you distributed. Make sure the speaker understands the questions to address. Give pairs a chance to pull their chairs to a space apart in the room. With an uneven number, you may pair up with the extra person. (You will still need to monitor the time.) Remind pilgrims that you will ring a bell or chime at the halfway point so they can stop, answer the questions on the handout, and then change roles. Practice holy listening.

After the exercise, invite the group to come back together to discuss briefly their experience as listener and speaker. What did people learn through this exercise? (They may refer to their notes on the back of the handout.)

➤ Naming: Reflections on Head2Heart (15 minutes)

Instead of the usual Naming questions, we will continue the experience we have begun with holy listening. Have the pairs spread out again. Ask each pair to look back at their index cards from the beginning of the exercise and decide on something that will mark them as traveling companions throughout the week—something beyond committing to pray daily for each other (that's a given). For example: stopping at the same time each day to pray; getting together sometime during the week; doing the daily exercises and readings in the Participant's Book at the same time each day.

Then give each pair two tea light or votive candles to light. Ask them to sit side by side, looking toward the candles, and pray for each other. They may choose to pray silently, pray for things coming up in their week, or simply repeat the Jesus Prayer for each other ("Lord Jesus Christ, Son of God, have mercy on _Name_").

Gather the pilgrims back together to reflect on the practice of being a spiritual friend and having a traveling companion. Encourage each pair to take their candles home and light them each day as they remember their fellow pilgrims.

➤ Blessing and Sending Forth (10 minutes)
See page 121 for instructions.

HOLY LISTENING REFLECTION SHEET

In this exercise you listen deeply to another person and share honestly. Remember that your speaking and listening always take place in God's loving presence.

As the Speaker

Take this time to talk honestly about where you have struggled in your pilgrimage this week, and then where you have sensed God's presence or felt God's absence.

As the Listener

Practice listening with your heart as well as your head. Along with the meaning of the words spoken, what feelings or mood do gestures, manner, or voice convey? How does the speaker's tone help you to interpret or understand the spoken words?

Feel free to nod, smile, or gesture in response, but try not to talk unless you are asking a clarifying question ("Did you mean . . . ?") or affirming with simple acceptance ("I see." "Ah." "Mmmm.")

The Process (15 minutes)

- Decide who will speak first. Take a moment to recall silently that you are in God's presence.
- Let the speaker talk and the listener listen for five minutes. (Chime will sound at end.)
- Take a minute at the chime to note on the back of this handout how you felt in your role and what you discovered.
- Reverse roles. Speak and listen for another five minutes.
- At the chime, note on the back of the page words or phrases that describe what you felt and learned.
- Take a few minutes to compare notes with your partner.

(over)

Holy Listening
Review Questions

For the Listener

- When were you most aware of God's presence (in you, in the other person, between you) in the midst of the conversation?

- What was the greatest challenge of this experience for you?

For the Speaker

- What was the gift of the conversation for you?

- When were you most aware of God's presence (in you, in the other person, or between you) in the midst of the conversation?

Adapted from *Exploring the Way: An Introduction to the Spiritual Journey* (Nashville: Upper Room Books, 2005), 79–80. Used here by permission; permission is granted to make one copy for each participant.

Week 3: Spiritual Guides

Preparation for the Meeting

1. See page 117 for additional notes about leader preparation.
2. Prepare the materials: In addition to materials listed on page 118, for the Head2Heart portion of the meeting, you will need: *Star Wars Episode IV: A New Hope* DVD; TV and DVD player; blank note cards, stamped envelopes, and pens.

Remember to help the pilgrims understand that repetition the Welcoming and Sending Forth prayers is purposeful. As you repeat them week after week, you will find that particular prayers, scriptures, and practices begin to sink from your head to your heart, forming you spiritually in the process.

➤ Welcoming (5 minutes)
See page 118 for instructions.

➤ Noticing: Listening to Your Life (15 minutes)
See page 119 for instructions.

➤ Moving from Head2Heart (30 minutes)

THE HOW-TO

Say something like:

One of the blessings of a spiritual pilgrimage is traveling with those who have covered more miles than we have. Relating to older, wiser pilgrims in our lives adds richness to the journey. They are guides and listeners—wise not because they have all the answers but because they have learned to ask the right questions. They have already walked through valleys and on mountaintops that we will encounter. Sometimes these traveling companions are called spiritual directors or spiritual guides. Our relationship with them can be formal—with a mentor or counselor, for instance—or casual, such as with a grandparent, minister, or neighbor. These traveling companions can help us recognize God's action in our lives and discern what God is calling us to do.

Exercise

Begin your time together by watching a movie clip that provides an example of mentoring. View Scenes 17 and 18 of *Star Wars Episode IV: A New Hope*.[4] After viewing the scenes, use these questions to explore how Obi-Wan (Alec Guinness) acts as a mentor.

- How does he act?
- What does he do?
- What characteristics make him a good mentor?

Next, invite each pilgrim to identify older, wiser traveling companions who are in their lives now or have been in the past. Encourage them to think beyond their youth or campus minister. Ask them to name one such person along with something they learned from that companion about life and God.

Give each pilgrim a stamped envelope and note card. Now invite people to think a little more about how the traveling companion they've identified has blessed them. What do they remember most clearly? Conversations? Time spent together? Words of wisdom? Ask them why they are thankful for this companion. Then ask pilgrims to write a personal message to their companion, thanking that person for what they have learned from his or her wisdom and presence.

When they have finished writing and put the note in the envelope, ask pilgrims to hold their envelope in the palms of their hands and offer a prayer of thanksgiving for the wisdom and presence of "older and wiser" traveling companions. Either collect the envelopes to mail or have the pilgrims mail them this week.

➤ Naming: Reflections on Head2Heart (15 minutes)

See page 121 for instructions.

➤ Blessing and Sending Forth (10 minutes)

See page 121 for instructions.

Preparation for the Meeting

1. See page 117 for additional notes about leader preparation.
2. Prepare the materials: In addition to materials listed on page 118, for the Head2Heart portion of the meeting, you will need: copies of the General Rule of Discipleship and the Sample Covenant handouts (pages 140 and 141) for the group.

➤ Welcoming (5 minutes)

See page 118 for instructions.

➤ Noticing: Listening to Your Life (15 minutes)

See page 119 for instructions.

➤ Moving from Head2Heart (30 minutes)

THE HOW-TO

Say something like:

Over the past few weeks we have learned about saints from our history and tradition, identified saints in our midst, and been challenged by the lives of saints. A beautiful image of our *interdependence* is a stand of redwood trees. The trees' roots are not particularly deep for their tremendous height, but the roots intertwine in a way that makes them strong for one another; their interconnected roots allow the trees to stand. As the redwoods support one another, we also support one another.

A powerful image of the *source* of our life is the vine of Christ. In John 15:5 Jesus says, "I am the vine, you are the branches." We want to be branches that bear good fruit, but sometimes we get disconnected from the source of life.

A wonderful practice in our Christian heritage actually links the image of the vine and the image of the redwoods. It's called *accountable discipleship*, and it helps us stay connected to the vine of Jesus and at the same time stay interconnected with one another.

You will lead an abbreviated accountable discipleship meeting with the group. Start by introducing the General Rule of Discipleship:

The General Rule of Discipleship in the Methodist tradition offers a vision of balanced and consistent discipleship.

Pass around copies of A General Rule of Discipleship (found on page 140); ask everyone to read the brief paragraph at the top and look at the diagram below. Provide some background:

The early Methodist societies helped people find the path that leads to life through a General Rule emphasizing "works of mercy" (doing all the good you can, avoiding all harm) and "works of piety" (praying, searching scripture, fasting, Christian "conferencing" or conversation, being temperate, and receiving Holy Communion).

Today covenant discipleship (or CD) groups use the General Rule of Discipleship that calls for discipline in four areas: worship and devotion, justice and compassion.

A CD group begins by working together to form a rule of Christian discipleship that has meaning for the members. The group meets weekly for one hour for mutual support and accountabililty. Ask everyone to look at A Sample Covenant that was written by one group (on page 141).

Now lead an abbreviated accountable discipleship meeting, following these steps:

- Divide the group into triads. Lead all triads from the front, giving specific time frames for each section.
- Ask pilgrims to keep in front of them the General Rule handout and the sample covenant. Explain that, for purposes of this meeting, the four categories of the General Rule will serve as a basis for the group to experience the accountable discipleship group model.
- Beginning with "acts of compassion," invite group members to take turns saying what that quadrant means for them and reporting on how they are doing with it. After all have shared related to the compassion quadrant, move on to the "acts of justice" quadrant, and so on.
- Help group members watch the time and move along in their reporting, but be careful not to rush anyone or to force a completion of all four quadrants in thirty minutes.

- Draw the meeting to a close by asking persons to indicate where they would like to deepen their discipleship in the coming week and areas where they need the prayers and support of fellow pilgrims.

You may want to suggest that members of the group consider forming a Covenant Discipleship group as a way to continue in fellowship and account-ability at the conclusion of this pilgrimage experience.

➤ Naming: Reflections on Head2Heart (15 minutes)
See page 121 for instructions.

➤ Blessing and Sending Forth (10 minutes)
See page 121 for instructions.

A GENERAL RULE OF DISCIPLESHIP

To witness to Jesus Christ in the world,
and to follow his teachings through
acts of compassion, justice, worship, and devotion,
under the guidance of the Holy Spirit.

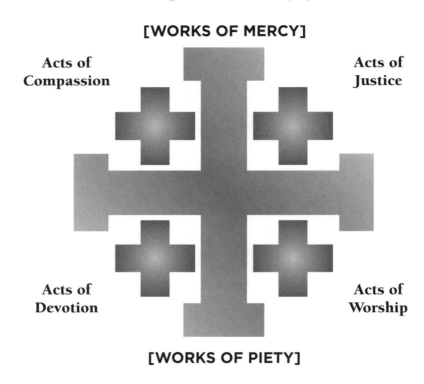

[WORKS OF MERCY]

Acts of Compassion

Acts of Justice

Acts of Devotion

Acts of Worship

[WORKS OF PIETY]

From *Companions in Christ: A Small-Group Experience in Spiritual Formation, Participant's Book* (Nashville, Tenn.: Upper Room Books, 2001), 298. Reprinted by permission; permission is granted to make one copy for each participant.

SAMPLE COVENANT FOR A
COVENANT DISCIPLESHIP GROUP

Knowing that Jesus Christ died for us and that God calls us to be disciples of Jesus Christ, we desire to practice the following disciplines in order that we might know God's love, forgiveness, guidance, and strength. Under the guidance of the Holy Spirit, we pledge to follow the teachings of Jesus through the following acts of compassion, justice, worship, and devotion.

ACTS OF COMPASSION

- We will be helpful to others in need or distress at home, church, and school.
- We will thank someone each day for small acts of kindness received.

ACTS OF JUSTICE

- We will speak out against prejudice when and where we recognize it.
- We will help recycle earth's precious resources at home, school, and church.

ACTS OF WORSHIP

- We will attend worship and Sunday school regularly.
- We will take Communion monthly when possible.

ACTS OF DEVOTION

- We will pray each day, including Covenant Discipleship members in our prayers.
- We will read a chapter of the Bible each day.

We make this commitment, trusting God's grace to work in us. We know that we are children of a loving God and that if we fail, we trust God's grace to forgive us and to help us have the strength to grow in our faith.

_____   _____
Date   Signature

The Way of Pilgrimage: Leader's Guide copyright © 2007 by Upper Room Books.
May be reproduced for group use.

Week 5: Walking with Those on the Margins

Preparation for the Meeting

1. See page 117 for additional notes about leader preparation.
2. Prepare the materials: In addition to materials listed on page 118, for the Head2Heart portion of the meeting, you will need: newsprint, markers, Bibles, paper and pens, copies of the Daily Examen outline (page 145) for each participant.

➤ Welcoming (5 minutes)
See page 118 for instructions.

➤ Noticing: Listening to Your Life (15 minutes)
See page 119 for instructions.

➤ Moving from Head2Heart (30 minutes)

THE HOW-TO

Say something like:

So far our traveling companions include the saints, our spiritual friends; older, wiser pilgrims; and other church members. Today we are going to talk about the pilgrims we meet less frequently along the way. Those might include individuals who run a retreat house or lead a cathedral tour, people like Aunt Mildred, whom we see only at Thanksgiving, or the social outcast in class who dresses oddly and says little.

We will consider the question, *Who is God calling us to walk alongside in love as Jesus walked with all kinds of people in his day?* Through the practice of the examen we will explore how God's call leads us to reach out to other pilgrims on the path of life. We know the blessing of intimate communities (family, friends, small groups), but we are also part of a much larger community that offers both abundant resources and pressing needs.

Exercise

Ask the group members to identify fellow pilgrims Jesus may be inviting them to love or reach out to. Gather responses on newsprint and expand on possibilities. Share author Roberta Bondi's reminder that we can't fully love God without loving God's image: this includes you, the person next to you, and every other person—even enemies![5] Learning to love as God loves is challenging.

Next, invite the group to explore a few stories in which Jesus reaches out to people who were not accepted by polite society or were not highly regarded within the Jewish social order.

Form groups of three to four. Assign each a different passage:

Matthew 19:13-15 (little children)

Mark 1:40-45 (healing a leper)

Luke 19:1-10 (Zacchaeus)

John 8:1-11 (adulterous woman)

Have the small groups read through the verses and pay special attention to the traveling companions Jesus encountered along the way. Ask someone in each group to take notes in response to these questions:

- What did Jesus do when he met a companion on the margins of his society?
- How did the traveling companion respond?

After five minutes, bring the whole group back together. Ask each small group to share its answers and insights. What similarities do people see in Jesus' companions? in their responses? Discuss what image from these stories pilgrims might take with them into the week.

Now ask everyone to turn attention again to the newsprint list of potential fellow pilgrims. Invite a minute of quiet reflection on how each person might reach out to one such neighbor pilgrim.

Our ability to respond to neighbors comes from paying attention to the spirit of God in our lives. As we learn to listen to God consistently in daily life, we hear the call that comes through little nudges, inner whispers, the words of another, or a sense of divine prompting in ordinary events and relationships. Responding to this call can be called "practicing the presence of God" in daily life.

One way to practice the presence of God is through the spiritual discipline of daily examen. We're going to learn a little more about the daily examen and try one form of it. The examen gives us a way to become more aware of our daily call to be fully available to God. Here is the form we will try together now.

———≈≈≈≈≈———

Introduce and practice the daily examen. Start with this definition:

The Upper Room Dictionary of Christian Spiritual Formation defines *examen* as "a way of examining or assessing one's life before God on a regular basis."[6]

Distribute copies of the Daily Examen handout found on the next page. Allow a few minutes for participants to read it. Then invite the class members to try this form of self-examination for the next ten minutes.

If your group meets in the morning or early afternoon, ask participants to review the last twenty-four hours; if you meet in the late afternoon or evening, review the day.

➤ Naming: Reflections on Head2Heart (15 minutes)

See page 121 for instructions. In addition, ask this question: **How could the examen help us learn to walk with people "on the margins"?**

➤ Blessing and Sending Forth (10 minutes)

See page 121 for instructions.

DAILY EXAMEN

The examen, a form of self-examination, refers to a brief practice of reviewing the day's thoughts, feelings, and actions in relation to God's presence. This practice works best in the evening before you retire for the night but can be used at other times of day by reviewing the past twenty-four hours.

The version of examen described below is based on the teaching of Ignatius of Loyola and takes the form of direct prayer. Allow yourself to be guided by these prayers:

God, my Creator, I am totally dependent on you. Everything I am and have is your gift to me. Thank you for the gifts of this day. I praise you for your generous grace!

Holy Spirit, you work through time to reveal me to myself. Increase my awareness of how you are guiding and shaping my life, and make me sensitive to the obstacles I put in your way.

You have been present in my life today. Be near now as I reflect on these things:

- *Your presence in the people and events of this day*
- *Your presence in the feelings I experienced today*
- *Your call to me*
- *My response to you*

God, I ask your loving forgiveness and healing. What I most desire healing for today is _____.

Filled with hope and faith in your love and power, I entrust myself to your care, and affirm that you desire to give me _____ (the gift you most need).

Adapted from an unpublished work by Kathleen Flood, OP, Nashville, Tennessee, April 2000. Used by permission in The *Way of Pilgrimage: Leader's Guide* copyright © 2007 by Upper Room Books. May be reproduced for group use.

Week 6: Being a Traveling Companion

Preparation for the Meeting

1. See page 117 for additional notes about leader preparation.
2. Prepare the materials: In addition to materials listed on page 118, for the Head2Heart portion of the meeting, you will need: sheet of paper and pen for each person. On newsprint write the word HOLY in large letters and under it these three words: *blessing, joy, gifts.*

➤ Welcoming (5 minutes)
See page 118 for instructions.

➤ Noticing: Listening to Your Life (15 minutes)
See page 119 for instructions.

➤ Moving from Head to Heart (30 minutes)

THE HOW-TO

Say something like:

God not only calls us to have traveling companions on our pilgrimage but to *be* traveling companions. God calls us to listen, guide, pray, support, walk beside, and look forward with one another. We pilgrims are called to make the living Christ visible in this crazy, darkened world—to become ourselves an open gate to heaven, full of sanity, balance, and light.

Exercise

Explain that as we journey together we begin to recognize the holiness not only around us but in us and in those we walk beside. This is part of the gift—the blessing of pilgrimage. Hand out a piece of paper and a pen to each person. Tell pilgrims to write their name at the top of the paper.

Have everyone sit in a circle with their Participant's Book to use as a hard surface for writing. Each pilgrim will then pass his or her own paper to the person on the right. Invite the pilgrims to listen to God during a few minutes of silence as they look for the holy in the pilgrim whose paper they are holding. The holy includes the blessing, the joy, the gifts they see in one another (point to the words on the newsprint).

Then ask the pilgrims to write the holiness they see in the pilgrim named on the paper. When everyone has finished, people pass the papers to the right again. Now every pilgrim has a different paper. Repeat the process until everyone has written on every paper except her or his own. Then make sure each pilgrim has his or her own paper back. Give the group a few minutes to read and digest the holy traits that their traveling companions have named in them.

In closing, ask the pilgrims to look for any themes in the holiness others have named on the paper. Can they see this holiness in themselves? Reiterate that on pilgrimage we learn that we ourselves are holy ground. We are places where heaven and earth intersect, where the gate opens and God can be seen. So part of our practice as pilgrims is to recognize the holiness in other pilgrims and in ourselves, just as we recognize holiness in a cathedral, a saint, or in the world around us.

➤ Naming: Reflections on Head2Heart (15 minutes)
See page 121 for instructions.

➤ Blessing and Sending Forth (10 minutes)
See page 121 for instructions.

VOLUME 5
STEPPING INTO THE WORLD

Repeating Liturgy for Volume 5

You will use this section each week as you work through this volume. It lists all parts that repeat for every session. Review the materials you need to prepare by turning to the first page of each session under "Preparation for the Meeting."

LITURGY OF MEETING

Welcoming
Noticing: Listening to Your Life
Moving from Head2Heart
Naming: Reflections on Head2Heart
Blessing and Sending Forth

Preparation for the Meeting

1. *Prepare yourself spiritually.* Remember you too are a pilgrim on this journey. The best way to prepare for each gathering is to practice living as a pilgrim yourself. Pray specifically for each pilgrim you journey alongside and for God to be present in your time together just as God is present in places of traditional pilgrimage.

2. *Prepare the space.* The space in which you will rest, pray, and share together on your journey is as sacred as places of traditional pilgrimage (such as Notre Dame, the Vatican, or Canterbury). So claim the space as God's sanctuary by placing in it a candle, cross, piece of fabric, icon, or other symbol to remind the group that you gather in the presence of God and to communicate to each pilgrim, "Welcome to this holy place."

3. *Prepare the time.* Being familiar with the readings, exercises, prayers, and practices in the Leader's Guide will help the meeting flow more

smoothly; you will be more more confident in your guiding; and you will have more freedom to let the Spirit move.

4. *Prepare the materials.* Prepare ahead of time small blank pieces of paper rolled up into scrolls (an 8 ½ x 11 sheet of paper cut into equal quarters is a good size). Tie each scroll with a six- to eight-inch pieces of twine or yarn. These will be used in the Noticing exercise. You will need one scroll for every participant (including yourself) as well as pens and a basket to hold the scrolls. You will need index cards for the Blessing and Sending Forth segment, one for each person, including yourself. You will need Bibles and paper. Post closing body prayer and benediction on newsprint or PowerPoint. See each weekly meeting for necessary Head2Heart materials.

The Welcoming and the Noticing together comprise the opening prayer of the session. So as much as possible (especially as pilgrims become familiar with the pattern of the meeting and with the exercises themselves) try to allow the first to flow into the next. Speaking softly and calmly makes leading exercises easier and can facilitate the flow of the session. Gentle instrumental music in the background may also be beneficial.

Remember that each weekly gathering of the pilgrims is a respite on their journey. Just as towns, churches, and abbeys welcomed pilgrims in earlier times, welcome the group's pilgrims into the meeting and holy space you have created. Before the pilgrims arrive, be attentive to the space: light the candle, have materials set out and prepared, provide water for refreshment; include any elements that communicate: "Welcome! Welcome to this place along the way."

If your group is unfamiliar with this traditional call-and-response, you might introduce it as a way that some more liturgical churches begin prayer. The leader offers a blessing to all present, and the people respond with a blessing for the leader. After the call-and-response, offer a prayer of your choosing.

➤ Welcoming (5 minutes)

Offer water and talk quietly to the pilgrims as they arrive. Once every one has arrived and you are ready to begin, say something like:

Welcome. Welcome to this holy place on your journey. It's good to be here. It's good to have you here. Thank you for coming. Let's begin first by welcoming Christ into our midst and by praying for the time before us.

Lighting the Candle

After everyone has gathered and been welcomed, allow a little quiet (a holy pause) for everyone to settle. Invite a pilgrim to light the candle in the middle of the room.

Leader: The Lord be with you.

Other Pilgrims: **And also with you.**

A PRAYER FOR LIGHT FOR OUR JOURNEY

Lord God of our journey, the light of our path, you know the plans you have for us, plans to bring us hope and not harm. Plans that will lead us more fully into the life you have given us to enjoy and to love. Plans that will bring us more fully into who you have made and called each of us to be. Thank you for welcoming us into your presence and light as we gather to seek you with all of our hearts. Be found by us, O Lord God of our journey. Amen.[1]

➤ Noticing: Listening to Your Life (15 minutes)

One reason for gathering together weekly as pilgrims on the journey is to assist one another in looking back and taking notice. How was God present to people? And what baggage have pilgrims been carrying around? In this weekly opening exercise, pilgrims will practice looking back through the week. Together they will symbolically leave their "baggage" in a basket (during the time together); then they will name where they noticed God in their week. This exercise encourages being more fully present to God, to one another, and to themselves during the group meeting time.

THE HOW-TO

Begin with this explanation:

Now we will begin the Noticing part of our meeting. As we gather together here in this holy space, we want to take a moment and remember where our journeys have taken us this week.

Begin by looking back through your week, taking special notice of moments along the way when you felt most alive. When were you most blessed, joyful, or peaceful? We are often able to recognize God's presence through these kinds of moments.

(Pause for reflection.)

We also want to think about what "baggage" we are still carrying from our week. When I say "baggage," I mean all those things that fill up our minds and weigh down our hearts:

> things we are worried about
> things we have yet to do or yet to finish
> things that left us discouraged
> things that have us bouncing off the walls
> all those things that distract us in one way or another from being present in this place (not physically present—clearly, you're here—but emotionally, mentally, and spiritually present).

Let's pray. Close your eyes and settle yourself. Take a few deep breaths and let's practice a holy pause together. *(Take a minute or so for this holy pause; you'll know when the pilgrims are settled and ready to engage in the practice of noticing.)* I invite you, in your own way, to ask Jesus to go with you back to the beginning of this week. Recount your journey day by day through the week. If it helps, imagine yourself walking hand in hand with Jesus, looking at the places, the people, the activities, the interactions, the ups and the downs of your journey this week. Answer these questions:

> What brought me joy?
> For what am I grateful?
> What weighed me down this week?
> What drained me?
> What worried me?
> What stressed me out?
> When did I feel hope?

(Allow several minutes for the pilgrims to contemplate these questions.)

Now take one of these scrolls of paper, a pen, and a piece of twine. Unroll the scroll, write down the baggage from your week, and then reroll the scroll and tie with the twine. Place your scroll in the basket as an outward sign of inwardly setting aside your baggage in order to enjoy this holy place on your journey and have space to receive what God has to offer you.

(Allow a few minutes for pilgrims to complete this process.)

Let's share briefly one place on our journey this week where we noticed God through blessing, joy, peace, or any other experience. There may be several things in your week that you could share, but please keep it to one.

Allow each pilgrim, including yourself, to share one experience.

Touching Base on Readings/Exercises

So what did you notice this past week in the readings and the daily exercises? What do you remember? What stirred you? How did you experience God as you read and practiced the daily exercises?

➤ Moving from Head2Heart (30 minutes)

The intent of this sacred time is to provide space for the message of the daily exercises and readings to move from the mind to the heart—in other words, to move closer to God on this pilgrimage. This segment includes an exercise or practice the group does together. See each weekly gathering for instructions for each Head2Heart exercise.

➤ Naming: Reflections on Head2Heart (15 minutes)

Following the Head2Heart portion comes a time of "naming," in which each pilgrim—alongside companion pilgrims—has the opportunity to articulate and name her or his experience of God through the Head2Heart exercise. Naming is an essential part of the spiritual formation and growth of each pilgrim. Here dots are connected, lightbulbs come on, struggles are affirmed, and journeys intersect.

THE HOW-TO

After completing the Head2Heart exercise, ask the following questions. Have pilgrims answer as they are comfortable. (In the first couple of sessions in a volume, you might need to explain what "naming" is and why it's important.) Other more specific questions might naturally come from the specific exercise.

- What blessing do you take with you from the exercise we just completed? (That is, what did you learn? What will you take home or carry with you on your journey?)
- How did you experience God during the exercise? Or, how did you experience God's presence?
- How/where did you experience the holiness or goodness of God during our gathering today?
- How will these experiences of God encourage you on your continued journey?

➤ Blessing and Sending Forth (10 minutes)

Now it's time for the pilgrims to pack their bags, gather what blessings they have received from this holy space, and move out to continue their journey. Sending them forth to continue their journeys is as important as the welcome. Hand out index cards and pencils .

THE HOW-TO

Say:

The question before us today as we prepare to continue our journeys out in the world is this: Given all that we've shared, learned and practiced, what is God calling us each to do on our journey? Write down the first word or phrase that comes to your mind/heart as I ask this question. Don't think about it too hard; just answer and write it down. If you don't know, that's okay. Ask God to let you know what God's calling you to (write that down instead). When you're finished, go ahead and put the card in your pocket.

Let us stand in a circle and prepare to go out into the world. This time instead of facing inward, turn outward because in this phase of our pilgrimage we focus our attention outward, on the journey before us. And since pilgrims pray with their bodies—it's all about moving. We will close with a body prayer:

Placing both hands on top of the head, pray out loud:
> **God be in my head and in my understanding.**

Placing both hands over the eyes, pray out loud:
> **God be in my eyes and in my seeing.**

Placing both hands over the ears, pray out loud:
> **God be in my ears and in my hearing.**

Placing both hands over the mouth, pray out loud:
> **God be in my mouth and in my speaking.**

Placing both hands over the heart, pray out loud:
> **God be in my heart and in my feeling.**

Placing both hands on top of the thighs, pray out loud:
> **God be in my legs and in my moving.**

Placing open hands one on top of the other in front of the body, pray out loud:

God be in my hands and in my touching.

Placing both arms at the side of the body, hands open and turning outward, offering our life to God, pray out loud:

God be in my life and in my journeying.[2]

Conclude by praying together:

Almighty and eternal God, so draw our hearts to you, so guide our minds, so fill our imaginations, so control our wills that we may be wholly yours, utterly dedicated unto you and then use us we pray as you will and always to your glory and the welfare of your people; through Jesus Christ our Lord. Amen.[3]

Leader:	Let us go forth into the world continuing on *The Way of Pilgrimage.*
Other Pilgrims:	**Thanks be to God.**

NOTE: Make plans now for a Closing Pilgrimage and Retreat after this six-week session is over. Find the retreat model and preparation suggestions at www.companionsinchrist.org/leaders.

Week 1: A Unique Calling

Preparation for the Meeting

1. See page 149 for additional notes about leader preparation.
2. Prepare the materials: In addition to materials listed on page 150, for the Head2Heart portion of the meeting you will need TV and DVD player, Disney's *The Prince of Egypt* DVD.

You will notice that the Welcoming prayer and Sending Forth prayer are the same for each week in this volume. Repetition and rhythm are essential parts of the spiritual life. Each week we come as pilgrims from the chaos of life to this centering ritual. Help the pilgrims understand that this repetition is purposeful and necessary. As you repeat various elements week after week, you will find that particular prayers, scriptures, and practices begin to sink from your head to your heart, forming you spiritually in the process.

➤ Welcoming (5 minutes)

See page 150 for instructions.

➤ Noticing: Listening to Your Life (15 minutes)

See page 151 for instructions.

➤ Moving from Head2Heart (30 minutes)

THE HOW-TO

Say something like:

The story of Moses provides clear illustration of a man called even from birth by God. He did not hear the call until later in life, and even then he was hesitant to follow; yet God chose him and was with him throughout his life. Listening carefully to his story can help us refocus on where we are hearing God's call in our lives. Where are you hearing God's call? What are you hearing God calling you to be and do? That's what we want to explore as we continue our session. We're going to read Moses' story, watch some clips from *The Prince of Egypt*, and do some journaling as a way to discern our own call from God.

Read the scripture listed, view the scenes indicated below, then read aloud the related questions. Give the group a few minutes to journal their responses to the questions.

1. Read Exodus 2:1-10. Then watch chapters 1 and 2 (baby Moses in the reeds) from *The Prince of Egypt.*
    - How did God choose Moses and show him grace and love even before Moses could choose God?
    - Have you experienced a similar grace and love as a child?

2. Read Exodus 2:11-15. Then watch chapter 7 (meeting Aaron and Miriam).
    - What did Moses learn about himself? How did it change him?
    - Have you ever met someone or had an experience that taught you new things about yourself?

3. Watch chapter 12 (murder and fleeing from Egypt).
    - What did Moses fear? What was he running from? What do you think he thought he was running to?
    - Have you ever done something that you thought put you outside of your family's forgiveness or beyond God's love?

4. Read Exodus 3:1-15. Then watch chapter 15 (burning bush).
    - What did Moses have to do to see the burning bush?
    - Have you ever encountered "burning bushes"—a person, situation, or need so compelling that it caused you to turn from your daily routine to pay attention?

Ask pilgrims to pair up to share their reflections. Pose this further question: **What parallels do you see between Moses' call and your own?**

After five minutes, continue with this final opportunity for reflection:

Moses' call is persistent, holds his attention over time, calls him by name, and seems impossible. Yet it made him remember the compassion he felt for his people; it required dependence on God; and it conveyed God's assurance. Through the burning bush God called Moses forward to help others. When have you had similar experiences? Looking at your life in light of Moses' story, do any of you see a calling emerging in your life?

➤ Naming: Reflections on Head2Heart (15 minutes)

See page 153 for instructions.

➤ Blessing and Sending Forth (10 minutes)

See page 154 for instructions.

Preparation for the Meeting

1. See page 149 for additional notes about leader preparation.
2. Prepare the materials: In addition to materials listed on page 150, for the Head2Heart portion of the meeting, you will need: a copy of your own or another denomination's social creed or your church/organization statement of beliefs; a list of current top ten songs from www.billboard.com (under "Billboard Hot 100"); lyrics and/or clips from these songs; a means of playing the music.

Remember that the Welcoming prayer and Sending Forth prayer are the same for each week of this volume. Help the pilgrims understand that this repetition is purposeful and necessary. As you repeat them week after week, you will find that particular prayers, scriptures, and practices begin to sink from your head to your heart, forming you spiritually in the process.

➤ Welcoming (5 minutes)

See page 150 for instructions.

➤ Noticing: Listening to Your Life (15 minutes)

See page 151 for instructions.

➤ Moving from Head2Heart (30 minutes)

THE HOW-TO

Have on hand the social creed or beliefs statement you've selected and the top ten songs—either as a list or audio clips. Write the four tools (Scripture, Tradition, Reason, and Experience) on newsprint for display. Say something like:

Listening for God's call and presence in our lives takes practice. And we have to keep listening so we can know where we are going. How do we listen for God's call in our lives?

- We listen through scripture—by practicing *lectio divina*.
- We listen to our lives—by paying attention to their rhythms: Are we exhausted? peaceful? joyful? playful? prayerful?
- We listen by being aware—by practicing the examen, noticing where God is active in our lives and how we're responding.

These are all ways to listen to God. But to fully discern God's voice among the noises and mixed messages of the world, we need some tools:

- *Scripture:* Is what I'm hearing consistent with the essential message and spirit of the scriptures?
- *Tradition:* What has the church said through the ages? What wisdom do I gain from my wider church heritage (or denominational creeds and principles); from my ministers and mentors?
- *Reason:* God has given us the intellect to think through situations and issues with reason and critical thinking.
- *Experience:* In relationships with people, the natural world, and everyday circumstances we gain valuable insights and wisdom unique to our own experiences.

You can use these four tools to help you hear God's voice and the leading of the Holy Spirit in the difficult dilemmas of daily living. You can even use scripture, tradition, reason, and experience as you listen to your favorite music.

Exercise

To begin this exercise, review the fruits of the spirit in Galatians 5:22-23 (traits revealing that the presence of the Spirit). Then have the group name characteristics of God and of things that are holy. List fruits and characteristics on newsprint.

Using Billboard's Top 10 list of popular songs (www.billboard.com), have the pilgrims practice the art of discernment. They will sort through what they hear or read, listening for the voice of God. (Don't use overtly Christian songs because this is an exercise in discerning and listening for God through the world, not the church.) Allow twenty minutes for this exercise, and don't worry about getting through all ten songs. Direct the group to look through or listen to lyrics one song at a time with these goals:

- Find any phrases that point to God's character or lyrics that speak of holiness.

- Look for the fruits of the Spirit.
- Identify any themes that are consistent with scripture or with the great creeds and principles of the church.
- Pick out phrases God might wish to say to you.

Challenge pilgrims to practice "holy listening" whenever they listen to the radio or other media; "holy watching" as they watch TV or movies. Remind them that God is always speaking; the problem is we either aren't listening or get too distracted by other noise. We aren't "tuned in" to the signal.

➤ Naming: Reflections on Head2Heart (15 minutes)
See page 153 for instructions.

➤ Blessing and Sending Forth (10 minutes)
See page 154 for instructions.

NOTE: Encourage pilgrims to take the spiritual gifts inventory starting on page 72 of their Participant's Book or online at www.elca.org/youth/resource /inventory.html before the meeting next week. Let them know that the group will be using results of that inventory in next week's meeting. Those who are unable to do it before next week will have an opportunity to complete it during the meeting.

Preparation for the Meeting

1. See page 149 for additional notes about leader preparation.
2. Prepare the materials: In addition to materials listed on page 150, for the Head2Heart portion of the meeting, you will need: copies of the Spiritual Gifts Inventory and the Scoring Grid on pages 72–77 in the Participant's Book; journal prompt questions posted on newsprint; and a ball of yarn. Note that the alternative to the Gifts Inventory requires a Bible.

Remember to help the pilgrims understand that repetition the Welcoming and Sending Forth prayers is purposeful. As you repeat them week after week, you will find that particular prayers, scriptures, and practices begin to sink from your head to your heart, forming you spiritually in the process.

➤ Welcoming (5 minutes)
See page 150 for instructions.

➤ Noticing: Listening to Your Life (15 minutes)
See page 151 for instructions.

➤ Moving from Head2Heart (30 minutes)

THE HOW-TO

Say something like:

In order to answer God's call and continue the journey, we need to know ourselves. We need to know that we are called by name and beloved. We need to know that God places gifts in our pilgrim's satchel, just as Aslan in *The Lion, the Witch, and the Wardrobe* gave each child a unique and perfect gift that enabled him or her to fulfill a specific role in the journey. Our pilgrim's satchel is full of gifts God has bestowed on us. We get the privilege of exploring those gifts and using them for God's purposes.

Exercise

Ask how many have completed the Spiritual Gifts Inventory (either online or in their Participant's Book) and have got the results. For those who haven't done it yet, hand out a copy of the inventory and give them time to complete and score it with the Scoring Grid in the Participant's Book.

For those who do have the results of their inventory, post the following questions in the room as journal prompts. Let them respond to these while the other pilgrims complete their gifts inventory.

1. With whom or where do you share your gifts?
2. What keeps you from sharing your gifts?
3. What would strengthen these gifts in you?

Invite pilgrims to read aloud their gifts from the inventory and any reflections they want to share from their journaling. Be aware that some gifts may be sensed but not articulated by members of the group. Ask pilgrims to be sensitive and gentle with one another during the sharing time.

———※₩₩※———

In the closing activity for this portion of the meeting, each pilgrim can affirm her or his gifts and how they might be used in the world. Tossing a yarn ball from one person to another provides the structure for expressing the gifts. Hold up the ball of yarn and describe the game as follows:

Take this ball of yarn and—holding onto the end—toss it to another pilgrim across from you. As you toss, name a way you could use one of your gifts for the world. For example, "I can use my gift of singing to join the church choir" or "I'm good at schoolwork and love children, so I will tutor after school."

Hold the ball of yarn in silence and think for a moment or two before tossing it and naming your gift. Be sure to hold onto the string as you toss the ball to another pilgrim. We will be creating a web, demonstrating how our gifts are held together through Christ. We need one another (and each other's gifts) to remind us of our roles in the journey we share. Everyone must hold part of the web for the web to be complete, so everyone needs to name a gift and toss the yarn.

———※₩₩※———

ALTERNATIVE: Instead of using the gifts inventory, you may base the exercise on 1 Corinthians 12:4-11. Read the text and ask persons to identify their own gifts from this list. Use the same journaling exercise and move through the rest of the meeting as described.

➤ Naming: Reflections on Head2Heart (15 minutes)

See page 153 for instructions.

➤ Blessing and Sending Forth (10 minutes)

See page 154 for instructions.

NOTE: If you haven't started yet, make plans now for a Closing Pilgrimage and Retreat when this six-week session is over. Find the retreat model and preparation suggestions at www.companionsinchrist.org/leaders.

Week 4: Finding Our Own Pilgrim Path

Preparation for the Meeting

1. See page 149 for additional notes about leader preparation.
2. Prepare the materials: In addition to materials listed on page 150, for the Head2Heart portion of the meeting, you will need: various magazines to cut up; poster board cut in half (or oversized paper/cardboard of any kind) for each person; glue, scissors, colored markers; sticky notepads; questions posted on the wall; meditative music; tape for hanging posters.

➤ Welcoming (5 minutes)

See page 150 for instructions.

➤ Noticing: Listening to Your Life (15 minutes)

See page 151 for instructions.

➤ Moving from Head2Heart (30 minutes)

Read Ephesians 2:10 and Jeremiah 29:11 aloud. Then say something like:

To review briefly what we've explored in our last few meetings: we listen for God's call as we journey on, carrying with us assurance of being God's beloved, our satchel of gifts, and the holy habit of listening. Part of continuing the journey is finding the specific pathway—the plan, the individualized journey—to which God calls us. Finding this pathway involves discerning our vocation. The word *vocation* comes from the Latin word *vocare*, which means "to call."

When we talk about vocation we are not necessarily talking about final career plans or church-based ministry. Vocation does not equate to our jobs, what we study, or what we want to be when we grow up. A true vocation can be expressed through any of these. But God does have an irreplaceable role for each of us in this world.

Remember from your reading what the writer Frederick Buechner has said: our vocation is the place where our deep joy and the world's deep need intersect.[4] We're going to explore this idea through a collage exercise.

Exercise

In this exercise participants will begin exploring God's call for them. Set out materials for collages: various magazines to cut up, poster board cut in half (or oversized paper/cardboard) for each person, glue, scissors, colored markers, and sticky-note pads.

Invite pilgrims to consider the following questions, posted in the room, and ask them to find images in the magazines that represent some possible answers to these questions. They can create collages by gluing these images to the posterboard. Direct them to do this exercise quietly, without talking to others. You could play meditative music softly in the background during the activity.

- What brings you deep joy, energy, and peace?
- Where do you see deep needs in our world?
- What is God calling you to do?

Provide tape to hang finished collages on the wall, or otherwise display them where everyone can see them. Place a supply of sticky notes near each collage. Invite the group to listen as you read again Ephesians 2:10 and Jeremiah 29:11. Ask them to keep these words in mind as they view one another's collages. Now encourage the pilgrims to walk around the room in silence, looking at the collages. They may use the sticky notes to post comments, observations, or questions about each collage. Suggest that they might start their comments with "I notice that . . ." or "Have you ever considered . . ."

Invite each pilgrim to share his or her collage and some of the sticky-note responses. Then, together as a group, try to name the possible "pathways" God may be calling that pilgrim to pay attention to. Repeat this for each person. If you are running short of time, continue this process in the Naming portion of the meeting.

Close with a brief prayer asking God for continued help in perceiving our particular pathways.

➤ Naming: Reflections on Head2Heart (15 minutes)

See page 153 for instructions.

➤ Blessing and Sending Forth (10 minutes)

See page 154 for instructions.

Week 5: A Pilgrim's Vulnerability and Availability

Preparation for the Meeting

1. See page 149 for additional notes about leader preparation.
2. *Prepare the materials.* In addition to materials listed on page 150, for the Head2Heart portion of the meeting, you will need: copies of the reading on page 168; Play-Doh or modeling clay and votive candle or tea light for each person; matches, CD player and CD with soft music; affirmation on page 170 posted on newsprint.

➤ Welcoming (5 minutes)
See page 150 for instructions.

➤ Noticing: Listening to Your Life (15 minutes)
See page 151 for instructions.

➤ Moving from Head2Heart (30 minutes)

THE HOW-TO

Say something like:

As we are discovering, the call of the pilgrim is to become more and more available to God and to fellow pilgrims. This week we will explore how the quality of our response to God's call may depend more on how Christ works in and through our weakness than on how much we can do for Christ through our strengths. Our culture teaches us to rely on our strength of character, our skills, our talents for doing God's work. But the way of the cross invites us to see that God sometimes works more powerfully in and through our weakness.

Hand out copies of the following reading and invite one person to read each paragraph aloud for the group.

A READING ON WEAKNESS AND STRENGTH

Our affluent culture expects that there is a way to fix almost anything that is broken—broken bodies, broken hearts, broken possessions. It is difficult for many of us to see brokenness as a part of life.

Within the tradition of the Native American Medicine Wheel, life is seen as a circle, as a whole, incorporating birth and death, the peaceful dawn and the thundering storms, wholeness and brokenness. From the northern direction of the Medicine Wheel come the storms of life. It is the storms that bring us courage and wisdom and compassion. Our lives would not be whole without the storms.

Richard Rohr says, "The place of the wound is the place of the healing. The place of the break is the place of the greatest strength." Our Christian faith affirms this—that Christ's wounds are the place where God's healing touches each of us.

Perhaps the task for us today is to begin to see the gifts of our broken places. To find the opportunities to believe in the mystery of Christ's death, "to put our finger in the wound of Christ, our own wounds, and the wounds of each other"[5]

Pose these questions related to the reading:

- **Do you agree with the Native American tradition or Richard Rohr?**
- **Can you give an example of how a person's weakness can be his or her strength?**

Lead a brief discussion about 2 Corinthians 4:6-12.

- Read the passage, inviting people to visualize what Paul is saying.
- Ask pilgrims to share their understanding of the meaning of this passage. What are the characteristics and purpose of clay jars? What does the image of clay jars or pots say about us? about God?
- Be prepared to help pilgrims deepen their understanding of this image: Paul presents here a rich, even humorous, image of our lives as clay jars that are cracked, imperfect, and weakened by difficulties we encounter as we seek to respond to God's call. The purpose of clay pots is to carry something and not to be perfect for their own sake. Paul emphasizes that the clay pots are imperfect and cracked by the hard knocks of life. Their very imperfection allows the extraordinary power of God to shine through! Because we are cracked pots, "the life of Jesus may . . . be made visible in our mortal body" (verse 11, NIV).

Guide the group in a meditative process of creating clay jars. Give each person a ball of Play-Doh or modeling clay and a votive or tea candle. Say something like:

Spend some time shaping a "clay jar" that represents your life. Put in cracks and crevices, imperfections, weaknesses, or impressions representing experiences that make you who you are before God. You don't need to make a perfect pot. God wants a jar that allows the light of Christ to shine through it and from it. The one requirement is that your jar can hold a candle inside.

Let the Spirit lead you as you shape the jar. Make space for God in your hearts with this prayerful affirmation: "We have this treasure in clay jars."

You may want to play quiet music as background for this exercise. Conclude the creative time by asking participants to contemplate what they have made for a moment in silence. What does it mirror about their life and the light within? What would they like to share about their clay pot with the rest of the group? Gather together then and proceed with the following closing. (If your group is large, you may need to form more than one circle in step two below.)

- Invite participants to set their clay pot with the votive or tea candle inside on the table and light the candle.
- As you stand in a circle, invite everyone to share his or her precious, uniquely imperfect clay jar. Ask each to share briefly (one minute) about its features that either allow light to shine through or block the light.
- Following each person's sharing, you might lead the group in repeating an affirmation, such as this one based on Isaiah 60:1. These words can be printed on newsprint for all to see.

  (*Name*), **arise, shine; for your light has come, and the glory of the** LORD **has risen upon you.**

➤ Naming: Reflections on Head2Heart (15 minutes)

See page 153 for instructions.

➤ Blessing and Sending Forth (10 minutes)

See page 154 for instructions.

Week 6: Every End Is a New Beginning

Preparation for the Meeting

1. See page 149 for additional notes about leader preparation.
2. Prepare the materials: In addition to materials listed on page 150, for the Head2Heart portion of the meeting, you will need: examen questions posted on newsprint; access to a labyrinth and small symbolic tokens for pilgrims exiting the labyrinth; or, for Rules for the Road exercise, copies of What Helps Me Stay in Touch with God? worksheet (page 174), paper, pens; copies of A Litany for Pilgrim People (pages 175–76).

➤ Welcoming (5 minutes)

See page 150 for instructions.

➤ Noticing: Listening to Your Life (15 minutes)

See page 151 for instructions.

➤ Moving from Head2Heart (30 minutes)

THE HOW-TO

Say something like:

T. S. Eliot wrote that when we finish exploring and return to our starting point, we "know the place for the first time."[6] So what does life look like now after this pilgrimage of six weeks? The beauty of real-life pilgrimage is that it never ends. A flight home from one journey is simply the flight that begins yet another journey. We are a pilgrim people, all trying to get back to our spiritual home. The question is whether we choose to answer the call to continue to be pilgrims, being present to ourselves, our companions, those we meet along the way, and to the God of our journeys.

Exercise

Select either Walking the Labyrinth or Developing a Rule of Life for your concluding session's exercise.

OPTION 1: WALKING THE LABYRINTH

This week provides an excellent opportunity for your group to walk a labyrinth. A labyrinth combines the images of the circle and the spiral into a meandering but purposeful path. The labyrinth represents a journey to the heart of God and back again out into the world. Labyrinths have long been used as meditation and prayer tools. If your church does not have a labyrinth, search for one in or near your community at http://wwll.veriditas.labyrinthsociety.org.

Whether you have access to a labyrinth or not, begin your exercise today with the brief awareness examen below. Have the pilgrims reflect on this journey, noting in their journals what they have learned, gathered, and treasured along the way. Do this exercise in silence.

Examen Questions

- **What have you put in your satchels?**
- **What are you taking with you for the continued journey of life?**
- **What have you left behind—things you started out with but no longer need to carry?**

If you can walk a labyrinth, give the brief explanation below following the examen; then invite pilgrims to enter the labyrinth as they feel ready. Greet each person as he or she exits the labyrinth and present a symbol of that individual's personal pilgrimage. This might be a prayer bracelet or flip-flop charm. Choose something that represents a meaningful part of your pilgrimage together.

Labyrinth Orientation

There are three stages of the walk:

Purgation—is a letting go of the details of your life—an act of shedding thoughts and emotions that quiets the mind.

Illumination—is a place of meditation and prayer when you reach the center. You can stay at the center as long as you like to receive what is there for you.

Union—is joining God at work in the world as you walk out. As you walk the labyrinth, pray for empowerment to find and do the work you feel your soul reaching for.

Articulate these guidelines for the walk:

- Quiet your mind and become aware of your breath.
- Allow yourself to find the pace your body wants to go. You may pass people or let others step around you, whichever is easiest at the turns. Don't be in a hurry.
- The path goes both ways. Those going in will meet those coming out. Keep your eyes soft and your heart open. Do what feels natural.[7]

OPTION 2: DEVELOPING A RULE OF LIFE

Ask pilgrims to write down their "rules for the road" (a rule of life) as a guide for their continuing journey. You could bring these suggestions to the table:

- Daily prayer. When? How long?
- Weekly worship
- Reading and studying scripture/*lectio*/imaginative meditation
- Exercise (keeping the holy ground of our bodies healthy)
- Sleep (again the holy ground of our minds and bodies)
- Time with traveling companions (older/wiser as well as peers)

After initial discussion of these rules, expand the categories by inviting reflection on the open-ended statements listed on the following page. (You may post the statements or give each person a copy of the worksheet). Allow time for pilgrims to journal; then invite sharing around responses to these statements. Ask how they might help expand our rules of the road.

➤ Naming: Reflections on Head2Heart (15 minutes)

See page 153 for instructions.

➤ Blessing and Sending Forth (10 minutes)

A special service of commissioning takes the place of The Blessing and Sending Forth. It appears on the pages following the worksheet.

WHAT HELPS ME STAY IN TUNE WITH GOD?

I hear God more easily when I . . .

I am reminded that I am on a pilgrimage when . . .

I am peaceful when . . .

I am joyful when . . .

Use the following litany in place of the Blessing and Sending Forth for this final session.

A Litany for Pilgrim People

With readings from The Message *(Isaiah 43:1-4) and* New International Version *(Psalm 84:1-2, 4-5) and responsive reading based on Ephesians 3:16-21*

Leader: Listen to the prophet Isaiah, speaking God's heart for the people.

But now, GOD's Message,
   the God who made you in the first place, Jacob,
   the One who got you started, Israel:
"Don't be afraid, I've redeemed you.
   I've called your name. You're mine.
When you're in over your head, I'll be there with you.
   When you're in rough waters, you will not go down.
When you're between a rock and a hard place,
   it won't be a dead end—
Because I am GOD, your personal God,
   The Holy of Israel, your Savior.
I paid a huge price for you:
   all of Egypt, with rich Cush and Seba thrown in!
That's how much you mean to me!
   That's how much I love you!
I'd sell off the whole world to get you back,
   trade the creation just for you."

Pause for a few moments of silence.

All: **You are our God, our Abba and our Redeemer. You have called us. You know us by name. You long for us, and we belong to you.**

Leader: "How lovely is your dwelling place, O LORD Almighty!

All: **"My soul yearns, even faints, for the courts of the LORD; my heart and my flesh cry out for the living God.**

Leader: "Blessed are those who dwell in your house; they are ever praising you.

All: **"Blessed are those whose strength is in you," whose hearts are set on the pilgrim's way.**

Leader: Lord, we are your pilgrim people.

All: **And we are called to follow Jesus, our companion, our guide, and our way.**

Leader: Yes, we are a pilgrim people trying to find our way back home.

All: **Home, to our God, our Creator and Keeper.**

Leader: We know our hearts will always be restless and never satisfied

All: **Until they find their home in you, Lord.**

Leader: So we commit our way to you, Lord God.

All: **We commit our hearts, our minds, our souls, and our lives to following you and the pilgrimage before us.**

Leader: Remind us that it is in you, our abiding presence, that we live, we move, we breathe, and we have our being.

Pause for a few moments of silence.

Leader: May your Word continue to guide us along the pilgrim's path;

All: **And may prayer open before us the gates of heaven so that we might live in communion with you.**

Leader: Thank you for blessing us with companions on this journey, those we see and those we see no more.

All: **Let them be a help on our pilgrimage through this world.**

NOTE: Before leaving, remind pilgrims about the date for your Closing Pilgrimage and Retreat. Find the retreat model and preparation suggestions at www.companionsinchrist.org/leaders.

NOTES

Introduction

1. Paragraphs 1 and 3 of this section are from an unpublished booklet on pilgrimage liturgy by Sally Chambers for youth pilgrimages she leads.

Volume 1

1. Body prayer used in Blessing and Sending Forth portion of weekly meetings is adapted from the *Sarum Primer*, 1558. (Copies of the Sarum Primer are available on microfilm in academic libraries.)

2. Henri J. M. Nouwen, "Our First Love," excerpt from a lecture at Scarritt-Bennett Center, Nashville, Tennessee, February 8, 1991.

3. Janet Wolf, "Chosen For . . .," in *The Upper Room Disciplines 1999* (Nashville, Tenn.: Upper Room Books, 1999), 128.

4. Saint Augustine, *Confessions*, trans. R. S. Pine-Coffin (Harmondsworth, England: Penguin Books, 1961), 177–78.

5. *A Longing for Holiness: Selected Writings of John Wesley*, ed. Keith Beasley-Topliffe (Nashville, Tenn.: Upper Room Books, 1997), 35–37.

6. Remember that motion pictures are protected by copyright laws. Both for-profit and nonprofit organizations, including churches, are required to have a public performance license to show movies, which include purchased and rental videocassettes and DVDs. More information is available from Christian Video Licensing International (888-771-2854).

7. Stages of walking the labyrinth based on description found at http://www.gracecathedral.org/labyrinth.

8. T. S. Eliot, "Little Gidding" Part V, in Four Quartets, in *T. S. Eliot: The Complete Poems and Plays 1909–1950* (New York: Harcourt Brace Jovanovich, 1971), 145.

Volume 3

1. From The Book of Common Prayer (New York: The Church Hymnal Corporation, 1977), Collect for Guidance, 100.

Volume 4

1. Adapted from The Book of Common Prayer, 250.

2. See www.myhealthclinic.org/Christina_Verneuil.shtml

3. *The Upper Room Dictionary of Christian Spiritual Formation* (Nashville, Tenn.: Upper Room Books, 2003), 244.

4. *Star Wars Episode IV: A New Hope,* film directed by George Lucas (1977).

5. Roberta C. Bondi, *To Love as God Loves: Conversations with the Early Church* (Philadelphia, Pa.: Fortress Press, 1987), 27.

6. *The Upper Room Dictionary of Christian Spiritual Formation*, 99.

Volume 5

1. Prayer written by Sally Chambers.

2. Adaptation of a prayer in the Sarum Primer, 1558.

3. Collect for Guidance from The Book of Common Prayer, 832.

4. Frederick Buechner, *Wishful Thinking: A Seeker's ABC*, rev. ed. (San Francisco: HarperSanFrancisco, 1993), 137.

5. Richard Rohr, *Breathing under Water*, audiocassette, as quoted in Beth Richardson, "The Broken Places" in *alive now!* (May–June 1991), 15.

6. T. S. Eliot, "Little Gidding" in *T. S. Eliot: The Complete Poems and Plays,* 145.

7. Adapted from labyrinth guidelines found at http://www.scarrittbennett.org /programs/labyrinth.aspx

IN THE INTRODUCTION

The Introduction is adapted from CIC Leader's Guide, rev. ed. (2006), 13–24.

IN VOLUME 1

Head2Heart exercises adapted from CIC Leader's Guide, rev. ed. (2006), 36–37 (Week 1), 41–43 (Week 2), 49–52 (Week 3).

IN VOLUME 2

Head2Heart exercises adapted from CIC Leader's Guide, rev. ed. (2006), 62–65 (Week 1), 68–70 (Week 2), 84–85 (Week 5), 62–65 (Week 6).

Head2Heart exercise in Week 5 adapted from Companions in Christ Participant's Book (2006), 96.

IN VOLUME 3

Head2Heart exercises adapted from CIC Leader's Guide, rev. ed. (2006), 90–91 (Week 1), 100–02 (Week 3), 112–13 (Week 4), 107–08 (Week 5).

IN VOLUME 4

Head2Heart exercise in Week 2 adapted from *Exploring the Way: An Introduction to the Spiritual Journey Leader's Guide* (Nashville: Upper Room Books, 2005), 77–80.

Head2Heart exercise in Week 4 adapted from CIC Leader's Guide, rev. ed. (2006), 170–72.

A General Rule of Discipleship on page 140 originally appeared in Companions in Christ Participant's Book (Upper Room Books, 2006), 298.

Head2Heart exercise in Week 5 adapted from *Exploring the Way: An Introduction to the Spiritual Journey* Leader's Guide (Upper Room Books, 2005), 85–89.

IN VOLUME 5

Head2Heart exercise in Week 5 adapted from CIC Leader's Guide, rev. ed. (2006), 130–33.

An Annotated Resource List from Upper Room Ministries

The following books, resources, and Web sites relate to and expand on the subject matter of the five units in *The Way of Pilgrimage*. As you read and share with your group, you may find some material that particularly challenges or helps you. If you wish to pursue individual reading on your own, or if your group wants to follow up with additional resources, refer to this list. Books published by Upper Room Books include the order number in parentheses. Upper Room Customer Service may be reached at 800-972-0433 or order online at www.UpperRoom.org/bookstore.

VOLUME 1—CHOOSING PILGRIMAGE

1. *The Godbearing Life: The Art of Soul Tending for Youth Ministry* (Upper Room Books, #858) by Kenda Creasy Dean and Ron Foster is a lively spiritual primer and practical guide for those who pastor young people. Dean and Foster rechart a course for youth ministry through the classical spiritual disciplines of the church. The book identifies families, congregations, and mentor relationships as the "holy ground" where young people are most likely to say "Yes!" to God.

2. *devozine* and *devozine Guide for Mentors and Small Groups* help teens develop a lifetime pattern of prayer and spiritual reflection by ordering *devozine*, an exciting, eye-catching devotional written by youth and youth leaders. Designed to link teens with their peers and help strengthen their faith, each issue includes scripture, prayers, feature articles, reflection questions, full-color art, and much more.

3. *Companions in Christ: Exploring the Way, An Introduction to the Spiritual Journey* (Participant's Book) (Upper Room Books, #9806) and (Leader's Guide) (#9807) will help you understand and deepen your experience of God. You'll be able to ask the questions of faith in a safe place. You'll discover (or rediscover) a way of grace, joy, and peace—indeed, the way of Christ himself.

4. *Soul Tending: Life-Forming Practices for Older Youth and Young Adults* (Nashville, Tenn.: Abingdon Press, 2004).

5. *Spiritual Literacy: Reading the Sacred in Everyday Life* by Frederic and Mary Ann Brussat (New York: Simon and Schuster, 1998).

6. *Under Her Wings: Spiritual Guidance from Women Saints* (#943) by Kathy Bence grew from the author's heartfelt longing for a deeper spiritual life. This book offers excerpts from the writings of five women saints and biographical sketches about each, as well as scripture readings, the author's meditations, questions for reflection and journaling, and prayer exercises. Through Bence's journey and observations you can discover wisdom from the past to illuminate your present.

7. *The Upper Room Dictionary of Christian Spiritual Formation* (Upper Room Books, #993) edited by Keith Beasley-Topliffe provides a basic introduction to Christian spiritual formation: a guide to great teachers of the past and present, to important topics in Christian spirituality, and to ways of praying and leading groups in prayer and spiritual growth. Whether you're just beginning to pay attention to the spiritual life or are helping others as a friend, pastor, or spiritual director, here's a good place to start seeking information about spiritual formation.

8. *You Gave Me a Wide Place: Holy Places in Our Lives* (Upper Room Books, #1002) by Paul E. Stroble intersperses personal stories with those about the sacred places of Hagar, Jacob, Christ, and other biblical figures. The exercises and readings are designed to help us identify where God's presence has "widened" (or made sacred) a place in our lives. Includes a six-week guide with prayers and questions for enriching small-group study.

9. Chrysalis. Chrysalis, a program ministry of The Upper Room, offers spiritual renewal to young people through a three-day experience and follow-up. Participants spend three days in worship, prayer, fellowship, creative expression, recreation, singing, and discussion. For more information, see www.upperroom .org/chrysalis.

VOLUME 2—THE BIBLE: PILGRIMAGE TRAVEL GUIDE

1. The 1979 Book of Common Prayer (New York: Oxford University Press, 2000).

2. *Shaped by the Word: The Power of Scripture in Spiritual Formation*, rev. ed., (Upper Room Books, #936) by M. Robert Mulholland Jr., considers the

role of scripture in spiritual formation and challenges you to move beyond informational reading to formational reading of the Bible. Mulholland demonstrates how your approach to scripture will in large measure determine its transforming effect upon your life. He examines the obstacles often faced in opening ourselves to God's living Word. You will find this a helpful resource as you examine daily patterns of attentiveness to God through scripture, and you will expand your learnings about formational reading.

VOLUME 3—PRAYER: HEART OF THE PILGRIMAGE

1. *365 Meditations for Young Adults,* ed. Sally D. Sharpe (Nashville, Tenn.: Abingdon Press, 2002).

2. *Breathing Under Water: Spirituality and the 12 Steps,* Richard Rohr, (Cincinnati, Ohio: Saint Anthony Messenger Press, 1989).

3. *Creating a Life with God: The Call of Ancient Prayer Practices* (Upper Room Books, #9855) by Daniel Wolpert goes beyond the rote prayers that so many of us have experienced and found wanting. In fact, Wolpert admits that his own frustration with the formula prayers and his unsettled longing immediately after college led to his search for a different kind of prayer, one that's "a deep conversation with God beginning with communion and leading to transformation." An appendix offers step-by-step instructions for practicing the Jesus Prayer and the prayer of examen, for walking the labyrinth, and more.

4. *Journaling: A Spiritual Journey*, rev. ed. (Upper Room Books, #866) by Anne Broyles offers stories, guided meditations, and questions to help you enrich your relationship with God through spiritual writing. Journaling includes practical advice for journaling and sufficient space for practicing each of the six methods of journaling the author outlines: from the events of daily life; in response to scripture; with guided meditations; from dreams; in response to reading; and from conversations or dialogues.

5. *The Soul's Passion for God: Selected Writings of Teresa of Ávila* (Upper Room Books, #828) edited by Keith Beasley-Topliffe shares the life of Teresa of Ávila, the prolific Spanish sixteenth-century nun, mystic, and celebrated writer. Included are portions from *The Book of Her Life, The Interior Castle,* and *The Way of Perfection*, all from perhaps the most noted and readable contemporary translation available.

6. *Way to Live: Christian Practices for Teens* (Upper Room Books, #975), edited by Dorothy Bass and Don Richter "invites you into a community of people who don't just go with the flow," say the editors. "This community's image of 'the good life' is not about having lots of stuff or being more successful than other people. Instead, it's about getting involved in the loving, challenging life of God." Journey with eighteen teens and eighteen adults as they try to find a way to live that keeps them involved in what God is doing in their lives and in the world.

7. *Openings: A Daybook of Saints, Psalms, and Prayer* (Upper Room Books, #9850), by Larry James Peacock, is a prayer book for every day of the year for people who don't normally think about using a prayer book. Move closer to God one day at a time by reading the Psalms and practicing prayer in ways you may not have imagined before.

8. *Praying Together: Forming Prayer Ministries in Your Congregation* (Upper Room Books, #979), by Martha Graybeal Rowlett, looks at the most popular and creative ways in which people are praying together in local churches today. Rowlett describes twenty-two prayer models with practical plans for implementation and other tips for those looking to develop inspirational prayer fellowship.

9. *Forty Days to a Closer Walk with God: The Practice of Centering Prayer* (Upper Room Books, #9904), by J. David Muyskens explores centering prayer, sometimes viewed as too mysterious, too escapist, too hard. Through Muyskens's insightful guidance, you'll explore a simple, biblical practice of prayer that leads to a deep communion with God and encourages a way of life motivated by the divine, perhaps untapped, Presence at the center of your being.

10. www.d365.org

Passport, Inc., and The Samuel Project produce the d365 devotional series. Passport's seasonal devotional sites, Journey to the Cross and Following the Star, help readers journey through Lent and Advent. These series are written especially for students and seek to provide reflections on themes that impact our faith journey.

11. www.labyrinthcompany.com

Beginning with their first Chartres Replica labyrinth built in 1995, The Labyrinth Company has been dedicated to promoting the widespread use of this meditation device.

12. www.micahprays.com

MICAH stands for Minnesota Institute of Contemplation and Healing. MICAH creates, supports, and develops programs and environments for the practice and study of spiritual formation and leadership, healing and the arts. As a contemplative Christian undertaking, MICAH provides a sacred space within which to create a life with God.

13. www.sacredspace.ie

This Web site invites you to make a "sacred space" in your day and spend ten minutes, praying as you sit at your computer, with the help of on-screen guidance and scripture chosen specially every day.

14. www.taize.fr/en

Taizé, in the south of Burgundy, France, is the home of an international, ecumenical community, founded there in 1940 by Brother Roger. The brothers are committed for their whole life to material and spiritual sharing, to celibacy, and to a great simplicity of life. Today, the community is made up of over a hundred brothers, Catholics and also men from various Protestant backgrounds, from more than twenty-five nations.

Since the late 1950s, many thousands of young adults from many countries have found their way to Taizé to take part in weekly meetings of prayer and reflection. In addition, Taizé brothers make visits and lead meetings, large and small, in Africa, North and South America, Asia, and in Europe, as part of a "pilgrimage of trust on earth."

VOLUME 4—COMPANIONS ON THE PILGRIMAGE

1. *Gathered in the Word: Praying the Scripture in Small Groups* (Upper Room Books, #806) by Norvene Vest. Using the classic spiritual practice of *lectio divina* or "divine reading" in the context of small, intimate prayer groups, Vest shows how this devotional and prayerful reading of the scriptures leads us to a deeper understanding of and relationship with God.

2. *Finding a Spiritual Friend: How Friends and Mentors Can Make Your Faith Grow* (#857) by Timothy Jones takes a fresh look at the Christian tradition of having a spiritual friend to guide, support, and encourage us in our faith journey. Using his own personal experience and stories from scripture,

the author describes the dynamics of guidance and accountability offered through a spiritual friendship. Jones convincingly portrays how our own formation is interwoven with other people in the faith community and how we can help one another in listening and responding to God.

3. *A Mile in My Shoes: Cultivating Compassion* (Upper Room Books, #9815) by Trevor Hudson issues a challenging charge to pay attention all around us and to engage in the spiritual disciplines that enable us to see, hear, and respond to the living Christ in our midst. In the dark period of South Africa's history, the author developed an eight-day experiential program called The Pilgrimage of Pain and Hope. He designed it to enable comfortable, young middle-class South Africans to reflect on the meaning of their faith and discipleship within the harsh and oppressive sociopolitical realities of their nation. Through the three ingredients of Encounter, Reflection, and Transformation, pilgrims learn to be present wherever they are, with whomever they meet, and whatever they see as they go about their daily tasks.

4. Spiritual Types Test and Discussion Guide. See www.upperroom .org/methodx/thelife/test.asp. Take the online quiz to help you learn about yourself and have some fun. Also available: a small-group study based on the Spiritual Types Test, the *MethodX Spiritual Types Test Discussion Guide* helps identify spiritual types—sage, lover, mystic, or prophet—and what they mean to our faith lives.

5. *The Riches of Simplicity: Selected Writings of Francis and Clare* (Upper Room Books, #834) edited by Keith Beasley-Topliffe depicts these thirteenth-century Italian saints through biographical vignettes as well as prayers, letters, and other spiritually rich writings from their remarkable lives.

6. *Together in Love: Covenant Discipleship with Youth* (Nashville, Tenn.: Discipleship Resources, 1999; order #DR271) by David C. Sutherland.

7. *Jesus, Our Spiritual Director: A Pilgrimage Through the Gospels* (Upper Room Books, #9876) by Wendy Miller brings the Gospel texts to life as a continuing conversation between Jesus and his disciples—then and now. Using a groundbreaking narrative approach, she demonstrates the deep biblical roots of spiritual direction in the ministry of Jesus, his disciples, and Christians today.

8. *Yours Are the Hands of Christ: The Practice of Faith* (Upper Room Books, #867) by James C. Howell. In this book you'll find ways to apply faith to your

daily life and find ways to make your commitment to Christ evident in today's world. By considering all that Jesus did with his hands as a teacher, a healer, and a compassionate servant, Howell challenges readers to be the hands and feet and love of Christ in the world.

9. *Kindred Souls: Connecting Through Spiritual Friendship* (Upper Room Books #9903) by Stephanie A. Ford is for individuals, prayer partners, or small groups who want to deepen the friendships they already have and open themselves to new friendship possibilities God offers. This book helps people find practical ways to develop and nurture spiritual friendships.

10. www.sdiworld.org

Spiritual Directors International is a global learning community of people from many faiths and many nations who share a common concern, passion, and commitment to the art and contemplative practice of spiritual direction.

VOLUME 5—STEPPING INTO THE WORLD

1. *God Goes to College: Living Faith on Campus* (Upper Room Books, #987) by Thomas C. Ettinger and Helen R. Neinast mines the authors' years of experience as campus chaplains to produce this companion for young adults trying to make sense of life, college, and vocational choices. Their reflections will help students recognize the need for grounding in God through prayer and spiritual practices throughout the college years.

2. *Companions in Christ: The Way of Transforming Discipleship* (Participant's Book) (Upper Room Books, #9842) and (Leader's Guide) (#9841) by Trevor Hudson and Stephen D. Bryant invite you on a journey to experience more deeply what it means to live as a follower of Christ. Understand the meaning of spiritual formation and how it leads to a spirituality that's authentic and grace-filled. Reflect on what your faith means in terms of who you are, how you must change, how you deal with pain, and how you relate to others. Be challenged to live the whole gospel by authentically connecting spirituality with discipleship.

3. *What About God? Now That You're Off to College: A Prayer Guide* (Upper Room Books, #655) by Helen R. Neinast and Thomas C. Ettinger helps young adults find a closer relationship with God during the changes, challenges, and

opportunities of college life. Compiled by two campus ministers, *What About God?* is a devotional prayer book divided into weekly themes focusing on relevant and contemporary issues, including independent living, sexuality, and embracing doubt. Each week includes an opening prayer, scripture readings, reflection, excerpts from spiritual writings, journaling ideas, and closing prayer.

4. *Living Your Heart's Desire: God's Call and Your Vocation* (Upper Room Books, #9805) by Gregory S. Clapper. Clapper goes beyond the usual career counseling formula, explaining why it's more helpful to understand the theology behind work, calling, and human freedom. He offers a variety of visions of what it means to lead a life of Christian faithfulness in all realms of existence. You'll be equipped to understand yourself as a Christian in the workforce as well as understand how to be content—no matter what you do for a living—among the discontented. Easy to read and relevant to today's economy and world (with many references and lessons from movies).

5. www.wondervoyage.com

Wonder Voyage Missions can be expressed in one exceptional idea: *Pilgrimage*. This nonprofit organization is dedicated to providing the modern-day sojourner with the unique opportunity of pursuing the heart of God in extraordinary locations, through unparalleled opportunities.

6. www.youthineurope.com

Youth in Europe is a Catholic youth pilgrimage company and committed to providing opportunities for groups and individuals to open their hearts to the grace of God through adventurous and faith-building pilgrimages to Europe, America, and World Youth Day.

MEETING NOTES

MEETING NOTES

....

....

....

....

....

....

....

....

....

....

....

....

....

....

....

....

....

....

....

....

....

....

....

MEETING NOTES

....
....
....
....
....
....
....
....
....
....
....
....
....
....
....
....
....
....
....
....
....
....
....

MEETING NOTES

. . . .

. . . .

. . . .

. . . .

. . . .

. . . .

. . . .

. . . .

. . . .

. . . .

. . . .

. . . .

. . . .

. . . .

. . . .

. . . .

. . . .

. . . .

. . . .

. . . .

. . . .

. . . .